the scented home

For Aurélia, who shares our passion for fragrance, and for Dora.

First published in the United States of America in 2002
by UNIVERSE PUBLISHING
A Division of Rizzoli International Publications, Inc.
300 Park Avenue South
New York, NY 10010

2002 2003 2004 2005 2006/ 10 9 8 7 6 5 4 3 2 1

Printed and bound in France by Pollina, Luçon - n° L85966-C

ISBN 0-7893-0687-5

the scented home

text **Laura Fronty** + photography **Yves Duronsoy**

universe

Contents

Of the five senses, smell has the closest thing to the full power of the past.
Smell really is transporting. Seeing, hearing, touching, tasting are just not
as powerful as smelling if you want to take your whole being back for a second
to something.... The good thing about a smell-memory is that the feeling of
being transported stops the instant you stop smelling, so there are no after-
effects. It's a neat way to reminisce.

Andy Warhol, *THE Philosophy of Andy Warhol (From A to B and Back Again)*

A home is made up of colors, materials, furniture, and objects that create a
particular atmosphere and impart a sense of well-being. But it is above all
scents, composed of different elements, which harmonize with each other to
compose the most personal of olfactory impressions. The aroma that greets
you when you push the door open. The aroma that remains imprinted on the
memory forever.

For some people what lives on in the memory is linked to smells of polish,
fruit, soft fabrics; to fragrances emanating from wardrobes, drawers, or even
a mother's handbag. For me the scent of memory is one of distant perfumes,
of dreams of other places, evoked by certain fragrances of sandalwood and
essence of tuberose, blended with a geranium carrying the scent of rose.
When I come across these scents again, I cannot stop myself from thinking
of the woman who wore them, like the woman whom Gauguin described in his
manuscript written in Tahiti, *Noa-Noa*: "One of those women who exude this

mixture of animal odor with the scent of sandalwood and the tiare flower."
Recalling a Tahitian woman he had painted, he elaborated, in the caption to one
of his paintings: "She had a flower behind her ear, which listened to her scent."
With the passing of time, this fragrant reminiscence has become the very
essence of my happy childhood. Today all I need to do is half-open the drawer
of a dressing table to rediscover the apartment where we lived in those days
and its atmosphere of yesteryear.

Some very tenacious scents are capable of permeating books, leather, fabrics,
or paper, and lingering for many years. I remember a trunk stored in the attic,
which we used in the 1930s. It still gave off the fragrance of a 'sachet powder'
by the perfumer Piver, with which a refined grandmother would scent the
interior of her luggage. I have kept the little stoppered bottle with cut-off
corners that she used to use—it still contains a few traces of powder, mingling
like a form of nostalgia linked to the past.

Scents from the past

Thus we also found at his home all kinds of things that would burn slowly—candles, wooden plaquettes, and scented ribbons.… And then, in addition, scented sealing wax; perfumed letters; lovers' ink made from rose oil; morocco leather writing cases; white sandalwood penholders; small, cedarwood boxes and caskets; pots-pourris and dishes for placing flower petals in; yellow copper incense holders; small dishes and little crystal bottles with their stoppers cut in amber; perfumed gloves; handkerchiefs; small sewing cushions stuffed with nutmeg flowers, and wallhangings imbued with musk, for perfuming rooms over a period of more than a hundred years. Patrick Süskind, *Perfume*.

It was not by chance that Patrick Süskind chose an eighteenth-century setting for his book's terrifying hero, Jean-Baptiste Grenouille, so obsessed with his quest for the perfect perfume that he is prepared to murder for it. The inventory of what you could look for in those days as regards scented objects and accessories reveals this dazzling period, which loved perfumes and was more passionate about scents than any other era—strong, musky perfumes masking the foul-smelling exhalations of daily life; light, floral perfumes used by Queen Marie-Antoinette to recreate the illusion of a natural paradise; perfumes for the skin; perfumes for the house diffused by precious pieces of porcelain, filled with potpourris.

In the past authentic perfumes extracted from plants were used for sprinkling around the house and for perfuming clothes, in order to hide other odors due to poor hygiene. Up to the second half of the nineteenth century, it was in effect necessary to mask nauseating smells that issued from bodies, clothes, houses, and the street.

Vinegar of the four thieves

1l (1¾pt) spirit vinegar
50g (2oz) lavender
15g (½oz) marjoram
15g (½oz) wormwood
15g (½oz) absinthe
15g (½oz) sage
15g (½oz) peppermint
15g (½oz) rue (*Ruta graveolens*)
10 cloves
10g (¼oz) ground angelica root
1 pinch camphor
90 proof alcohol

Steep all the aromatic ingredients in the vinegar for 15 days, inside a bottle stoppered with a cork.

Filter, then add the camphor, dissolved in a little 90 proof alcohol.

This antiseptic vinegar can be used by soaking a handkerchief with it or it can be burned to fumigate a room where a sick person is resting.

You can also use it in bathwater or as an invigorating rub, when it is cold and you are stiff and aching. This recipe is kept in the Museum of Old Marseille, also known as "the Museum set with diamonds."

According to historian Alain Corbin, author of *Miasma and Daffodil*, a remarkable book about odors and how society perceives them, the olfactory revolution took place in the eighteenth century, when the smells emanating from other people became really unbearable. "The fact that odors issuing from oneself became more clearly defined, more intensely felt, only provoked a sense of repulsion for the smells emanating from others, smells of the bodies of the rich rotting in churches, the smell of the sweating throng in crowded public places." The solution was to resort to perfumes of a rare intensity that you spread throughout the house, thanks, in particular, to potpourris or apples of amber (with musk as principal ingredient in those days, contrary to what the name suggests). Handkerchiefs soaked in 'vinegar of the four thieves' were also used, or small bouquets of strongly aromatic plants—even fatal ones that you risked inhaling when plague was rife—which were supposed to fight unhealthy emanations.

In accordance with popular belief at that time, herbs and perfumes did possess a genuine therapeutic value. A hygienist quoted by Corbin affirmed that "myrrh, camphor, camomile flowers, and cinchona, all scented substances, prove to be the most effective antiseptics." Another recommended "sniffing a red carnation and scattering angelica powder over clothes." Corbin recalls that "to arm oneself with an olfactory shield, to smell strongly, to sniff the aromas of your choice, constituted for a long time the most effective of sheaths against deadly poison." Thus burning scented lozenges, using essential-oil burners, wearing perfumes, or breathing in the scents of fresh plants was as much about concern for basic hygiene as about pleasure.

THE VINEGAR OF THE FOUR THIEVES This recipe would have been given by thieves who had escaped from the great plague that ravaged Marseille in 1720 and claimed more than 100,000 victims in Provence and the South of France. The epidemic had been carried from the East by a ship loaded with fabric, and spread by rats and fleas. The city's leading merchants had concealed the growing epidemic and exempted the vessel from a period of quarantine because of the Beaucaire fair, the largest trade fair in the South of France, which was to be held some days after the ship's arrival.

For a long time this aromatic vinegar was considered a necessary element of a first-aid kit and every family had some in their possession to disinfect the atmosphere. It was also supposed to prevent infectious diseases through simple fumigation. The original recipe comprises all kinds of aromatic plants and camphor.

APPLES OF AMBER OR POMANDERS In the sixteenth and seventeenth centuries the pomander became popular throughout Europe. Used like a jewel, it was worn suspended at the end of a cord or a chain and was invested with a function at once prophylactic and magic. Its smell was believed to be capable of fighting pervading putrid fumes—in Latin it was referred to as *pomum pro odore* (scented apple). But its spherical shape, resembling an apple or a pomegranate, was also symbolic and thus it served equally as an amulet against the forces of evil.

Hollow and pierced with holes, this pendant was filled with a strongly scented substance with a base of herbs and precious resins—among others, musk and ambergris, from which its name 'apple of amber' or 'pomander' derives. In the sixteenth century the pomander was prepared by mixing benzoin, ladanum (scented gum), storax, cinnamon, cloves, orris root from Florence, aloeswood, and valerian with musk; civet and ambergris as fixatives. All these ingredients were combined to form a paste, which was blended and rolled by hand into the shape of a ball, so that it could be enclosed in a pendant pierced with numerous holes. The majority of these pomanders were made from precious materials or metals, which made them genuine scented jewels.

Today wearing this magical object that the Renaissance attributed with every kind of virtue is no longer fashionable, but fruits (orange, lemon, or even a real apple) stuck with aromatic cloves are still very popular, especially in England and America, where they are used traditionally at Christmas. They are adorned with ribbons, hung from the Christmas tree or grouped together in a large bowl.

Present-day apple of amber

1 untreated orange
100g (4oz) cloves
2 tablespoons ground cinnamon
1 pinch ground mace
1 teaspoon orris root powder
1 large darning needle

Using a needle, mark out lines between the base and the top of the orange to form quarter segments on the peel. Following these lines, make a hole in the orange peel and stick a clove in the fruit. (You can also take off thin bands of peel with a peeler and stick the cloves in the flesh of the fruit.) Continue until the fruit is completely studded with cloves.

Pour the spices and the orris root powder into a large bowl or a dish and roll the fruit in it until it is completely covered with scented powder.

Cover the bowl and let the fruit steep for about 15 days, turning it over every day, until it is very dry (as if mummified) and imbued with many amber colors and sweet scents. To vary the fragrances you can substitute the orange with a lemon, a lime, an apple, or even a grapefruit (for the last, steep for three weeks to a month).

In Anglo-Saxon countries these scented fruits have a place of honor during end-of-year festivities. But it is a pity to deprive yourself of their rich scent for the rest of the year, because they suffuse the atmosphere of a room, a wardrobe, or a cupboard with a very agreeable fragrance.

Indispensable salt

You will need salt to produce certain very old potpourris, known as 'moist' (see the Rose potpourri recipe, page 23), in which the ingredients cure under layers of salt for weeks. Though less decorative than a dry preparation, these potpourris have a much stronger scent and can be hidden under flower petals.

POTPOURRIS This is the name given to scented preparations consisting essentially of rose petals. The custom probably dates back to antiquity, but it was from the eighteenth century onwards that it became really popular. Each mistress of a household—or almost—had her own recipe. Roses were its main element, supplemented by many other plants, as well as herbs and spices as fixatives.

The best potpourris are those you prepare with flowers, leaves, or aromatic roots and spices. Beware of the ready-made variety you can buy, which are artificially tinted and scented with synthetic essences such as essence of green apple or red fruits, likely to give a headache to lovers of natural fragrances!

What you can put into a potpourri

Aromatic plants
Use vervain leaves, lemonbalm, different varieties of sage (common sage, clary sage, pineapple sage), thyme, lemon thyme, oregano, wild thyme, different varieties of mint (peppermint, spearmint, bergamot-mint), wormwood, lavender, every variety of scented geranium, tansy, and santolina.

Scented flowers
Choose rose first, but also yarrow, carnations, monarda with the fragrance of bergamot, jasmine, honeysuckle, and orange blossom.

Unscented flowers
For color use the flowers and the dried petals of carnations, mallow, pink or blue delphiniums, marigolds, blue nigella; French marigolds, heather, hydrangeas and yellow and orange-colored potentilla.

Spices
Choose star anise for its very decorative shape and its aniseed aroma, cinnamon, nutmeg, mace, cardamom, vanilla, coriander, cloves, ginger, allspice, fennel, cumin, and caraway.

Fixatives
Use orris root powder, vanilla powder, cinnamon, and essential oils (rose, lavender, neroli).

In addition...
The peels and rinds of citrus fruits (orange, lemon, grapefruit) are always attractive. Also use other less common but heavily scented ingredients—pine buds, wood shavings, and cedar cones; balsam poplar leaves and buds with their aroma of incense; orris root or angelica root; and the roots of perennial geranium.

These recipes can be simply sources of inspiration for mixtures you can create yourself without scrupulously adhering to the proportions. Do not hesitate to combine all kinds of scented plants. Your nose will be your guide.

Green mixture

1 handful dried vervain
1 handful dried lemonbalm
1 handful dried rosemary
1 handful dried mint
1 handful dried lavender
½ handful lemon thyme
3 pinches rose geranium leaves
1 pinch mint-scented geranium leaves
    (*Pelargonium tomentosum*)
5 drops bergamot essence
5 drops benzoin essence
3 drops orange flower essence

Mix the plants and leaves well in a bowl and then add the various essences.

Spicy potpourri

60g (2½oz) dried lavender
90g (3½oz) dry rock rose or rosemary leaves
    and flowers
600ml (1pt) eau de cologne
zest of 1 orange
3 tablespoons orris root powder
1 tablespoon cinnamon powder
1 tablespoon mace
1 tablespoon ground allspice
3 drops scented geranium essential oil
3 drops lavender essential oil

Put all the ingredients into a covered container. Blend well, cover, and let stand for 12 hours.
    Uncover and place on a mantelpiece. With the heat of the fire, this potpourri will release a delicious aroma. This recipe is taken from *Natural Housekeeping* by Beverly Pagram.

French-style rose pots

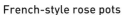

250g (9oz) *Rosa damascena* or
    Rosa centifolia buds
Cloves (1 per bud)
Orris root powder
Amber essence
Flower petals

Take buds from scented roses such as
the damask rose (*Rosa damascena*) or the
cabbage rose (*Rosa centifolia*).

Remove the green section of each bud
and plant a clove in the center. Allow to
dry over several days (about a week).

Roll the dry buds in orris root powder,
to which a few drops of amber essence
can be added.

Combine the dry buds with the flower
petals, selected for their perfume or their
color, in a dish or a large bowl. Sealed in a
pot, the buds may well have given rise to
the French expression *découvrir le pot aux
roses*, which means literally, "to discover
the rose pot"—in other words "to stumble
upon what's going on." When you lifted the
lid, a heady aroma emanated from the
mixture.

Rose potpourri

500g (1¼lb) dried damask rose petals
250g (9oz) salt
15g (½oz) ground nutmeg
15g (½oz) crushed cloves
15g (½oz) orris root powder
15g (½oz) ground cinnamon
15g (½oz) dried thyme

In a pot or a jar, alternate layers of salt
and rose petals mixed with spices and
thyme. Tightly seal the container. Allow to
steep for at least a month, stirring the
ingredients regularly. You can remove
some of this highly scented mixture and
add it to another potpourri to enhance its
aroma, or divide it among different bowls.
A few highly colored dried flower petals
are sufficient to cover this scented base,
which does not look very decorative.

If damask rose is not available, you
can use any variety of rose as long as
it is highly scented. Among the scented
varieties, I recommend the Piaget or
the Papa Meilland, which are gloriously
scented, modern roses. You gather their
petals once they have withered.

Spicy mixture

1 tablespoon aniseed
1 tablespoon crushed cloves
1 teaspoonful ground cinnamon
3 drops vanilla essence
1 tablespoon star anise
A few tonka beans (optional)
Cinnamon sticks for decoration
Benzoin essence

Mix the aniseed, cloves, and cinnamon
in a shallow dish. Distribute evenly the
vanilla essence, the star anise,and the
tonka beans (if you managed to buy some
at your local herbalist or at a perfumery).
To decorate, add the cinnamon sticks.

Finally, pour a few drops of benzoin
over this brown-colored mixture with its
warm scents, giving off both a vanilla and
an aniseed perfume.

Fragrant bouquets

In summer we shall treat the pampas grass with disdain, and we shall plant suffocating white lilies among the roses…, more imperious than orange blossom, more passionate than tuberose, these lilies that climb the stairs at midnight and come and find us when we are deeply asleep. Colette, *The Lady in the Photograph*.

Colette personified flowers. They are characters inhabiting the house and the garden, and she gives them a soul. They welcome us, accompany us, keep us company. In *Flora and Pomona* she evokes in this way a stroll along a path, defended by old lilacs, guelder-roses, and marshmallows, where the scents 'walk along slowly' and come alone to meet the walker, delegated by a peppery, yellow rose, lime blossom, and a large scarlet poppy.

Using all the natural world's scented plants is still today the simplest and most agreeable way to decorate and fill your home with fragrance. In this regard, do not be reluctant to let your imagination run wild, because anything—or almost anything— goes. To give pleasure to the senses, arrange flowers in your home in places where they will be shown to maximum advantage—on a bedside table, on a mantelpiece if the chosen composition will tolerate the heat from the fire, on a bookshelf, near a sofa or armchair that is your favorite spot for lazing…. And for a few seconds, you shall breathe in a whiff of happiness!

Winter eucalyptus

In winter all types of eucalyptus with their ash-green or golden-brown leaves, more or less rounded or pointed, make their appearance at florists. Towards the end of winter, you even find bouquets brightened up with flowers with silky red pompoms and very decorative cone-shaped seeds. A few leaves arranged on a plate with stones and small pebbles are all you need to create a scented decoration, as the rather peppery, pungent perfume of their resin fades very slowly.

HEADY PERFUMES Plants constitute a whole world of olfactory sensations, always different and ceaselessly renewed. But of all the flowers, without a doubt the rose possesses the richest perfumes. Do we not speak of the rose of a hundred perfumes? Indeed, there is not one rose perfume, but several, which are often connected to the color of the flower and are sometimes surprising.

Thus, with some white roses, perfumers distinguish the fragrance of hyacinth, the smell of the sea, and the aroma of aniseed. Red roses sometimes have a bouquet of wine, raspberry, strawberry, or blackcurrant leaf. Some amber roses emanate a whiff of jasmine, a swirl of tea, a taste of ripe apricot; while others evoke clove, capsicum, or citronella. At the same time—the world of plant scents is a strange one—peonies have a scent of rose.

Alongside these marvelous roses, certain highly scented flowers are called "the perfumer's despair," because, paradoxically, the perfumer can only reproduce their fragrance by virtue of his creative talent. Lily of the valley, lily, honeysuckle, lilac, and peony are some of the elusive beauties who can only live again through the magic of the imagination and by the marriage of natural and synthetic scents, sealed in a bottle.

Other flowers emanate such a strong perfume that they can provoke headaches. But not everyone suffers from floral perfumes in the same way. For some the tuberose is unbearable. For others it is the heady, sickly-sweet smell of blue hyacinths that upsets them, while the silent but pervading fragrance of large white lilies can sometimes even bring on a migraine.

BOUQUETS FOR HAPPINESS Bouquets do not always bloom in vases. Sometimes they also become delicate, scented jewels. In Yemen men and women adorn their heads with small perfumed bouquets that attract love, luck, and happiness. These bouquets are called *mushgur* and comprise pennyroyal, marjoram, and purple basil leaves. Sometimes a rose or a carnation is added for its color. Young newlyweds fix these bouquets in their hair before going to bed, as it is said that they help to ward off demons during the night.

In Tunisia and Morocco men often slip small jasmine bouquets behind their ears, for the sheer pleasure of inhaling the ineffable white scent, a real invitation to love.

Ideas for floral decorations

Grow hyacinths, which will make the short days of winter balmy and fill a room with their sweet fragrance.

Place a powdery mimosa branch and a very small bunch of violets, tightly bound by a collar of green ivy leaves, in a vase.

Breathe in the fragrance of daffodils, heralds of spring, or jasmine flowers, small stars with a white, pure scent.

Float a gardenia, jasmine, or magnolia flower in a small dish of water. Contemplate its matte, velvety whiteness and become intoxicated with its perfume.

Fill the house with armfuls of mauve lilacs and irises with silk petals, and with the fragrance of sweet violet.

Grow a handful of *Cosmos atrosanguineus* in your garden. Come autumn, you will rediscover the joys of making a bouquet from these strange small flowers, dark brown and velvet like the cocoa whose aroma they have borrowed.

Spread roses about the house for their colors, available in myriad shades, and their distinctive, individual fragrances—roses in profusion, combined with velvety, scented geranium leaves.

Dot about the house bouquets of fresh mint, wormwood, and absinthe, to relive the sensations experienced while strolling through an Eastern souk where herbs are sold.

Have fun making small bouquets of herbs with a selection of rosemary, chamomile, wormwood, sage, thyme, miniature roses, or small pinks, just like tussie-mussies—old-fashioned posies in a pretty, scented tangle.

Moss and rose arrangement

2 handfuls moss
2 handfuls scented roses
½ handful mace
½ handful green cardamom
1 handful scented geranium with rose-scented
    leaves (*Pelargonium fragrans*) or lemon-
    scented leaves (*Pelargonium citriodora*)
Rosewater or orange blossom water

Blend the moss, scented roses, mace, and cardamom in a dish. Place the scented geraniums on top of the fresh leaves. Gently moisten by spraying with a little floral water to deepen and soften the warmest parts of the moss.

This composition is inspired by a recipe given by Catherine Willis, artist, sculptor, and creator of perfumes, in *Perfumes and Flavors of the Home*.

Certain mosses and lichens are now rare, and permission is needed to collect them—and indeed more common kinds— on woodland walks, so it is wisest to look in garden centers if you do not have any in your garden.

Mosses and lichens

If you have mosses and lichens in your garden, you can collect small pieces and arrange them in a bowl or a shallow dish like a miniature Japanese landscape. You just need to moisten them each day with a spray to revive the aroma of the forest, of fallen leaves and moist earth.

Fragrant still-lifes

Pieces of glass smoothed by the surf and collected on the beach; round, sleek pebbles; a collection of stones and lichens: all of these can be transformed into still-lifes, to which you need add only a few drops of essence to bestow on them the magic of perfume. But be careful— essences are generally rather greasy and can stain the stones and pebbles. Add just a few drops of essence to the side that will stay hidden.

Table decorations

Of course, the violet can also be associated with feasts, intoxication, and passionate declarations of love. In Athens times of merriment or celebration were precisely the occasions when you were most likely to find it. Crowns of foliage were flecked with rosebuds, violets, lilies, or daffodils, so much so that they blended effortlessly with caresses, softly spoken words, and perfumed bodies.

Jean-Luc Hennig, *The Jerusalem Artichoke and Other Marvels.*

The notion of being surrounded by heady perfumes while tasting choice dishes seems sacrilege to the gourmets of our century. However, things were done differently in the classical era and it was unimaginable to hold feasts without rosewater fountains and a profusion of scented plants, to the extent that it sometimes made the guests light-headed! Athenians and Romans could not conceive of a banquet without flowers. They adored roses in particular, but also loved violets. The tables and floor were strewn with petals, and the guests dressed their hair with garlands and crowns of flowers, whose fragrances were supposed to disperse the heady fumes of alcohol. During the sumptuous banquets hosted by Nero in his palace, the Golden House (Domus Aurea), rosewater gushed forth from fountains and every divan was adorned with precious cushions stuffed with scented rosebuds, while a mist of flower water was exhaled from chinks made in the walls. Such floral extravagance reached its peak with the emperor Heliogabalus— on one evening he literally suffocated his guests under a cascade of petals tipped in abundance from an awning, which had ripped at the wrong moment under its excessively heavy load.

While the Middle Ages confined the use of flowers strictly to the realms of religion or hygiene, it preserved from ancient traditions the custom of strewing aromatic plants (lavender, rosemary, sweet flag—a kind of scented rush—basil), such as were common in Ancient Rome. This custom is sometimes observed in certain Mediterranean countries. Thus on Easter Sunday in Spain and Portugal the people walk upon a carpet of freshly cut lavender; while in Greece—in Hydra for instance—bundles of myrtle, laurel (sometimes woven to form crowns), or sage are preferred.

But it was in the Orient, undoubtedly through Byzantium and subsequently Constantinople, that the love of the rose remained almost intact. Even now, in the most modest dwellings there, you honor guests by presenting them with a ewer filled with rosewater, with which they can refresh their hands before and during a meal. Good food and fragrances can be compatible today, as long as the latter remain discreet. A sprig of lavender placed near a plate, a fingerbowl subtly decorated with flowers.... The fragrances of flowers, the aromas of spices, and scented herbs are welcome guests; with the fare, they contribute to the feast of the senses.

Scented dining

Place a delicately scented flower on the napkin of each guest.

Fasten the napkins with a tie, kept in place by a couple of star anise or alternatively tonka beans.

For a knife rest use vanilla pods, or cinnamon or liquorice sticks, gathered in small bundles and fastened with a length of raffia, or with a gold tie or a ribbon.

Beside each plate, place a small glass or a pretty eggcup, decorated with a tiny scented bouquet, comprising herbs, geraniums, and small flowers.

Decorate the base of the glasses with a circlet of ivy, rosemary, or lavender, enhanced by roses or violets.

Place small dishes of rosewater or orange blossom water at intervals on the table, and float petals of roses, red carnations, or peonies in them.

Use flower water in fingerbowls after a seafood or shellfish dish.

Hang the branch of a lemon tree, bearing fruits still a little green from the dining-room doorknob. Leaves rubbed between the fingers smell deliciously good.

Make sophisticated fingerbowls by laying in each bowl a sprig of jasmine, placed on a pebble, and floating vervain on the surface of the water.

Finish the meal with a coffee scented with orange blossom water, as it is sometimes served in North Africa; or with a 'white coffee'—a Lebanese infusion of orange blossom, scented with lemon rind.

As in India, offer your guests a blend of ground and colored, scented seeds (aniseed, cumin, cardamom), to freshen the mouth. For a more European version, you can also offer violet flowers or rose petals preserved in sugar.

In the beginning were wisps of smoke

The use, so ancient and widespread, of incense and perfume in churches, in every nation and religion, causes us to rejoice and arouses and purifies our understanding to render us more receptive to contemplation.Montaigne, *Essays*, Book One.

Since ancient times human beings have communicated with the gods through the medium of incense. Like herbs and perfumes, incense belongs to every culture and every great human civilization.

In order to forget that they were mere mortals, our distant ancestors needed only to burn leaves, barks, seeds, or precious resins, whose smoke rising to the sky, put them in touch with the divinities they honored by reciting incantatory prayers. The origin of the word 'perfume' can be traced to these practices—odoriferous substances *per fumare* (by means of smoke) destined to be reduced through smoking.

There is evidence in most mythologies of these sacred fumigations, born of the sap or bark collected from certain plants. These emanations had both a practical significance (to perfume and purify the atmosphere), and a ritual and symbolic one. They represented as it were the soul breaking free from the body to rise up to the gods.

Laden with almost magical powers, they freed human beings from their materiality. By offering them a way of concentrating and contemplating, these emanations also allowed them to attain a high spiritual and mystical plane more easily, and even reach a state of ecstasy.

The incense of the Yemeni

Even today, *bakhûr' adanî* is sold in the spice market in Aden. This is a mixture exclusively for women, in particular for lovers' trysts. It is composed of mastic, sandalwood, and aloeswood, from an exceedingly rare tree, originating in Asia, on which a parasitic mushroom lives, bestowing on the wood its exquisite aroma. Musk, rosewater, and sugar are added to these base ingredients. The mixture, reduced to a powder, is moistened with rosewater and then molded into small, irregular, brown- colored pebbles.

ANCIENT RITUALS In Ancient Egypt such a vast quantity of incense was used, that the plants collected in the whole of the Middle East, as far as Palestine and Syria, became no longer sufficient to honor the numerous divinities. Scented resins were offered to the gods at sunrise, midday, and sunset. This is why Egyptian sailors, in 5,000 BC, were the first to trace the route of what was later to become the Spice Road. Much later on, Queen Hatchepsout sent an expedition to the land of Pount, today situated between Djibouti and Cape Guardafui, in present-day Yemen. Some of the frescoes in the temple of Deir El Bahari, built by the queen, depict the exploits of these adventurers in quest of incense and everything they brought back to Arabia Felix, 1,500 years ago. "In summer, when the wind blows from the continent, aromas emanating from myrrh trees and other odoriferous trees are carried along by the wind, and reach that part of the sea that lies near by…. Those who have tasted the flavor of these fragrances believe they have tasted the food of the gods," the Greek historian Diodorus of Sicily related, evoking Yemen. In this legendary region, naturally suffused with the fragrance of balsam trees, cinnamon, and sweet-flag, highly prized plants were collected. Bitter myrrh, for example, with a lemon and rosemary fragrance, and above all *Boswellia carteri* (frankincense), the resin that, once heated, released what the Egyptians called the 'divine aroma': olibanum or white incense.

The Greeks, and then the Romans, made extensive use of incense (of lavender, rosemary, and, of course, an abundance of frankincense), both in the temples and on the occasions of grand ceremonies. Nero alone would have burned more incense for his wife's funeral than Yemen produced.

Sandalwood

The capital city of sandalwood is Mysore. It is just as much a perfume (sublime!) as a substance intended for incense, particularly in India, where it originates.

This highly fragrant oil is extracted from a tree, which is now protected since it is in danger of extinction. It is incorporated with sandalwood sawdust and then molded into small sticks that are burned. It is said that the smoke they give off is propitious for sensuality and for amorous relations.

Myrrh

Originating in Arabia, this is an amber resin, more or less dark in color, broken into small fragments to burn over charcoal.

In antiquity it was used for embalming ceremonies and was included in the sacred oils ritually used by the Jewish people. For the Ancients it symbolized the soul. It is said that myrrh is feminine (whereas frankincense is masculine), and that it stirs the powers of the imagination.

THE INSPIRATION OF THE DIVINE SPIRIT Hereafter, incense was no longer burned for Isis or Osiris, Jupiter or Venus, but it is often still an element of the realm of the sacred and the mystic.

In every Christian church with Eastern rites, mass takes place in an atmosphere of thick, sweet-smelling smoke. And you only have to attend a celebration of the Grand Mass at Easter in Spain to see gigantic, richly ornate censers descend from the ceiling of the cathedral or the church, spreading over the congregation a heavy, pungent fragrance that our forefathers associated with the Christian religion. Like Rimbaud, who, in *A Season in Hell* retained in his memory this "aroma of incense, so powerful; guardian of sacred herbs and spices, martyr confessor"…a blinding premonition of the fragrances he would breathe in later, on the way to Yemen, then to Ethiopia.

SACRED SMOKE, PROFANE SMOKE In Asiatic civilizations incense and ritual fumigations enhance both the realm of the spiritual and that of the profane. In Japan, the land of incense, there are some infinitely rare and precious substances, unknown by the Western world, like *Aquilari agalloche* wood or aloeswood (not to be confused with the succulent aloe plant that grows in Mediterranean regions). The Japanese consider this an inestimable treasure, and it is used for manufacturing the most precious incenses.

In Ancient Japan it was common practice to burn sticks of incense in front of samurai tombs (like an olfactory offering to the departing soul), or on the occasion of the tea ceremony, or even to perfume kimonos and women's hair. The women would fall asleep with the nape of their neck placed on an openwork headrest. As they slept, their hair became imbued with a slightly resinous perfume.

Curiously, the same customs are found in Yemen, where even today, women maintain the custom of scenting their clothes with aloeswood incense. They lay the fabrics down on a large wickerwork bell, inside which the perfume burner is placed. And when they emerge from the hammam, with their skin and hair still damp, they will also have exposed themselves to the aroma emanating from the smoke.

In the Japanese imperial court there were actual aroma tournaments, the *kôdô* or 'koh-do,' in which the participants had to recognize the main ingredients being burned in front of them. These incenses contained aromatic powders that had been extracted from plants, such as patchouli, camphor, benzoin, or cloves, blended with sawdust from scented woods such as sandalwood, chamaecyparis (cypress), aloes, or ginkgo.

In India sandalwood has always been a sacred plant. Its scented wood is ground to a powder that is burned in front of altars dedicated to Buddha and numerous gods. In the pre-Columbian era in Central America the Mayas burned aromatic herbs blended with copal, a red resin extracted, according to an ancient legend, from the Tree of Life—it yielded the very emanation of the divine spirit, materialized through celestial smoke. In North America the Native American Indians still burn wild sage during the celebration of their rites.

These customs and traditions illustrate an indisputable reality: the infinite diversity of ritual ceremonies in every human culture and civilization.

Frankincense

This is found in India, Africa, and Arabia. Over thousands of years the olibanum has become *the* incense plant, a universal substance that is simultaneously priestly, magical, and profane. It is sold in the form of pale yellow or very light amber drops, which must be burned in a heat-resistant metal or clay receptacle, over hot charcoal.

Benzoin

This is obtained from the sap of an Asiatic tree that grows in southern India, Indochina, Thailand, and Indonesia. The highly fragrant and milky-hued balm is extracted by making incisions in the bark. As it dries, it yields a kind of amber-tinted opaque resin, which is broken up into small pieces.

This marvellous substance is also used in the perfumery and beauty world because of its pleasant fragrance, which has a touch of amber and vanilla. It must be burned over charcoal. It is said that its emanations drive out gloomy thoughts, depression, and a tendency to gluttony!

Rose incense

Highly scented fresh rose petals or
  Moroccan rosebuds
Dried lavender
Orris root powder
1 300ml bottle (½pt) rosewater
Benzoin tincture

To calculate quantities start from the principle that roses should represent half of the mixture: for example, for 50g (2oz) roses, measure 25g (1oz) lavender, and 25g (1oz) orris root powder.

Pulverize the roses and lavender by pounding them in a mortar or using a blender. Add the orris root powder to this fragrant mixture and gradually moisten with rosewater and benzoin, so that you have a fairly thick paste, with which you can shape small 2cm (¾in) high cones. Leave them to dry for 15 days, then store them in a metal box, protected from damp.

Use these cones in the same way as Indian incense cones.

This recipe is adapted from a method given by Catherine Donzel in *Perfume*.

INCENSE, TEARS, POWDERS, AND RESINS Largely neglected since the 1970s, incense is enjoying a revival. It has lost its 'hippie' connotation and you can now find all kinds of subtle and sophisticated perfumes presented in an infinity of forms.

In the world of small incense sticks, tears, powders, and fragrant resins for burning over hot charcoal, it is not always easy to make your choice. The most widely available, for you to try depending on your mood, have a base of frankincense, myrrh, benzoin, or sandalwood. There are also a number of perfumed incenses that though not belonging to an authentic tradition, offer a very large selection of the most diverse scents—woody, flowery, or spicy. Some specialized companies market infinitely rare and precious substances such as *Aquilari agalloche* wood; they cost a lot more than ordinary incenses, but you need burn only one stick to make all the difference and to appreciate their delicacy and sophistication.

Generally, incenses composed entirely of powders and sawdust molded into small sticks, without the support of wood to hold them upright, are of a better quality than other kinds. Incense cones, originating from India, should be burned on a heat-resistant support designed for this purpose. Never place them directly on wood or any other flammable material, and be aware that they leave indelible brown traces afterwards.

Lozenges from the harem

100g (4oz) benzoin (available at herablists)
5g (⅛ oz) amber (available at Asian
 grocery stores)
5g (⅛ oz) sandalwood
15g (½oz) caster sugar or 5g (⅛ oz) saltpeter
Gum arabic per 100g (4oz) (available at
 herablists)

Mix all the ingredients, then shape them
into flattened balls, which you light with
a flame (gas, or fire in a fireplace). Then
leave to burn in a perfume burner or an
essential-oil burner made of thick metal.

Perfume for burning

30g (1¼oz) dried damask or Provins rose petals
20g (¾oz) dried lavender
40g (1½oz) orris root powder
15g (½oz) cloves
50g (2oz) storax
3 drops bergamot essence
2 drops cinnamon essence

The essential element of this recipe for
scenting the air in accordance with an old
English method resides in gathering all
ingredients.
 Rose petals, lavender, and orris root
powder, as well as essences, are available
from herbalists.
 Put all the scented ingredients into a
fire shovel heated until it is red-hot. As
they burn they will release delightfully
perfumed wisps of smoke.

PERFUMES FOR BURNING One chronicler recounts that during the Great Plague that devastated London during the year 1665 frankincense, sulphur, pepper, and hops were burned in some particularly badly affected districts; whereas in the rich residences that were still plague free they placed near the fire metal essential-oil burners containing aromatic substances sometimes infused in vinegar, whose vapors were supposed to possess disinfecting powers or even simply tobacco.

Later the prophylactic virtues of these incenses were associated with the pleasure derived from suffusing interiors with fragrance. From the seventeenth century, fashion followed the Orient in all its forms and the stories of travellers on their return from Constantinople, describing the famous Topkapi Palace and its beautiful odalisques, made ordinary mortals dream. We undoubtedly owe these lozenges for burning to this vogue for all things Turkish; the divine 'lozenges from the harem' were embraced by beautiful, elegant ladies of the day and gave them the illusion of being in the Orient. At that time the lozenges were prepared according to a traditional method. Today you can make them yourself (the only difficulty lies in assembling the ingredients), or burn a little amber and benzoin over charcoal.

Certain beauties of the day also made fashionable the old technique of the fire shovel, which was made white-hot, and into which they threw aromatic plant substances to spread a fragrance both pleasant and ephemeral, through a room. They also burned incense paper with a benzoin base, to disinfect the house and to fill it with fragrance. In this period there is no doubt that the divine was far from their thoughts.

Incense paper

Ordinary white paper
Potassium nitrate (saltpeter) solution,
   composed of 56g (2oz) saltpeter and the
   same amount of water
100g (4oz) benzoin powder
10g (¼oz) essence of myrrh (soak the myrrh
   in a glass of 90 proof alcohol)
5g (⅛oz) rose or scented geranium essence

First immerse the paper in the nitrate
solution. Mix the scented ingredients, then
immerse the paper to aromatize it. Leave
the paper to dry completely, then cut it
into strips or rectangles.

You can still find these narrow strips of
paper that, while burning slowly, give a
sweet smell to Siam benzoin, at hardware
stores and in certain specialized shops.
Their role is to scent the air but also to
fumigate it. At least this was what was
claimed until the early twentieth century,
when some encyclopedias of practical
living gave their readers recipes to make
them themselves. This one is fairly simple
to carry out, as long as you can obtain all
the ingredients.

PAPIER D'ARMÉNIK
TRIPLE

PAPIER D'ARMÉNIK

Good combinations

Invent your own recipe for scented essence. Take perfumed toilet vinegar that you have made yourself or from among the delightful brands you can buy at Dyptique in Paris, at Floris in London or New York, or at the pharmacy of Santa Maria Novella in Florence. Add some cloves, mace, star anise, long pepper (sold in fine grocery stores that specialize in products imported from all over the world), and a pinch of cinnamon. If you pour half a wine glass of this mixture into the water of a radiator humidifier, the atmosphere will be exquisitely fragrant.

Even more simple, concoct a kind of fumigation for the house by adding a few drops of essential oil or a vinegar preparation to a bowl of boiling water: the effect will be fleeting but still particularly pleasant.

It is imperative that you resist the temptation to burn a few drops of your own perfume or, even worse, eau de toilette, which has a high alcohol content. Their chemical structures are not intended to withstand strong heat, and they break down. Sometimes, the result is surprising and, frankly, unpleasant.

OILS AND ESSENCES These are undoubtedly the oldest means of scenting the atmosphere. In his book *Natural History*, Pliny the Elder mentions twenty-two kinds of perfumed oils designed to be burned in essential-oil burners or perfume burners. Scented plants such as oregano, galbanum with its warm aroma of cistus, coriander, juniper, "cypress, lentisk, marjoram, broom, iris, valerian, rose, myrtle, and bay," which grow in their wild state on every Mediterranean riverbank, were poured into olive oil, almond oil, nut oil, and opium-poppy or poppy-oil, which was impregnated with resins and sweet-smelling saps. In Crete one of the most valued plants for this use was the clary sage with its powerful aroma, blended with rose petals, lilies, or broom, which softened its bitterness. These oils had a sacred role like incenses, but were also used for everyday purposes around the home or for medical needs.

Today we have all kinds of oils and essences at our disposal (almost as many as there are perfumes to burn!) whose aromas are released when they are heated. The simplest method consists of pouring a few drops on a disc of asbestos or heat-resistant clay, which you then place over a bulb; when the bulb is switched on, the perfume permeates the whole room. However, please note: always put the disc soaked in essence over a switched-off bulb, and never pour oil or essence on a switched-on bulb—there is a risk of explosion. You can also pour the scented oil, mixed with water, into a small, heat-resistant dish and place it on a receptacle containing a small candle to warm dishes. Old teapots are perfect for this use, but there are also perfume burners available, that are specially designed to diffuse heated perfumes.

The fragrance of flames

I lit a fire, azure sky having abandoned me

A fire to be its friend,

A fire to find my way in the winter night

A fire to have a better life.

Paul Éluard, *Selected Poems*.

Native American Indians burn torches of sage, wormwood, and juniper at purification ceremonies. The branches are dried, and at the base they are stripped of their leaves. Bouquets are then made from them, with juniper in the center, surrounded by wormwood and sage. Each sheaf is tied with a cord, which fits tightly round it like a net. By simply lighting the end of it, and letting it smoulder for a few moments, the plants can be left to burn like incense.

With a little shrewdness and imagination, the flames we light in our homes can be as fragrant as these sacred fumigations. But it is not only the fire burning in the fireplace that releases an aroma. Many elements can burn, leaving the fragrant memory of their ephemeral passage in their wake: discs heated over a bulb, oils, and aromatic essences warmed in a perfume burner, eternal incense paper or even a Berger lamp more than a hundred years old. Not forgetting, of course, candles with a thousand perfumes.

FIREWOOD, FIRE OF JOY "The home we dream of is warm, never blazing. The warmth we dream of is always balmy, constant, unvarying. Through warmth all is profound.... The appeal of soothing warmth unites every intimate value," Gaston Bachelard wrote in *The Earth and Reveries of Repose*.

It is no coincidence that the word 'hearth' denotes the intimate, family space in the home, as well as the place where the fire is lit. The fire in autumn and winter bestows upon the house that aroma as familiar as any, where slightly pungent smoke and the scents from burnt wood and resin with a hint of tar combine. A fire that by itself gives both the most luxurious room and the most intimate bedroom the appearance of a glowing cave, where all that can be heard is the gentle crackling of a log, which smolders while whistling or gently hissing.

Certain types of wood, in particular resinous woods,are more fragrant than others. But they need to be watched closely as they throw out sparks and minute but very dangerous live embers when the fireplace is not equipped with a fireguard. The apple tree, the balsam poplar that gives out a scent of incense and benzoin, the hazel, the lime, the pear, the pine, the cedar, and the thuya are very aromatic.

Driftwood, washed up by the great equinoctial spring tides and found on riverbanks, releases a scent of the sea when it burns, with a hint of slightly resinous lavender. And in vineyard regions, the pleasure experienced in starting a fire with vine shoots remains unabated.

The fragrance of flames

If you have an old lilac in your garden that you wish to remove because it no longer produces enough flowers, or that throws out branches in disorderly fashion, cut up the trunk and branches into bundles of firewood that you can use to light a fire. The wood and the withered flowers release a very pleasant aroma as they burn.

In winter keep bouquets of withered roses; branches of eucalyptus and juniper; small branches of rosemary, fennel, thyme or sage, dried heather; and even orange, lemon, or clementine peel in a huge basket. Added to the live embers, they will burn very well and dissipate unpleasant smells, caused by humidity or poor ventilation.

If you have a garden with a laurel, prepare some garlands by threading the leaves on string. With lavender (or rosemary) branches, make some scented bouquets. These aromatic elements added to small pieces of kindling wood will sweeten the air while they burn. You can also use laurel garlands as decoration in a basket of pine cones or kindling wood.

Make the most of woodland walks by stocking up on pine cones. Arranged in a hamper or a basket, they will look very decorative before you use them as firelighters for autumn and winter blazes. To give them added appeal, pour a few drops of an essential oil between their scales: try vetiver, sandalwood, or cypress with woody scents. They will fill the room as well as the fire with fragrance (but watch out for sparks thrown out when you are lighting it).

Suffuse bundles of firewood with a pleasant aroma by soaking them with an essential oil of flowers, wood, or spices; or, even better, an oil designed for burning (one of those used over electric bulbs). To ensure that they become permanently saturated, put them in a tightly sealed box for two weeks. Then place these bundles in an attractive basket near the fireplace.

Good uses for candles...

For a dinner party, light the candle an hour before your guests arrive, then extinguish it so that the scent is detectable without being intrusive during the meal itself.

Never let a candle burn without supervision, and if it is standing in a glass container do not place it on a cold surface (marble, glass, or metal) when it is lit. When the candle has melted down and the wax has almost gone, the pot could well melt, owing to the difference in temperature between the glass and the material on which it is resting.

The scent of a candle starts to spread after a certain time, when the wax has melted evenly. If the wax melts in an uneven way, the wick is undoubtedly crooked. Reposition it with the blade of a knife so that it is straight, and also consider recutting it, so that it is not too long and does not char.

PERFUMED CANDLES Solid green in its glass jar, dressed in a bow of red satin, the Rigaud candle, created in the 1960s, emanated sophisticated, woody scents of cypress. It was one of the first creations of the genre and offered a delightful alternative to people who until then had only used the Berger lamp (more than a hundred years old today), whose wick was dipped in alcohol, or even age-old incense paper.

Perfumed candles arouse real passion now and you can choose from among scents evoking the forest as well as a kitchen garden, a flower garden, or an orchard. Some even whet the appetite for sweet things with aromas of chocolate, coffee, tea, spice bread, or ripe fruits. However, remember that 'notes' of warmth, woods and spice are the best ones to 'attach' to the heat of the flame. Fresh, green scents are less tenacious and more transitory. At Dyptique, a respected store where the most marvellous scented candles are sold (there are more than 40 perfumes), certain notes of scents are advised in accordance with certain rooms of the house. For the drawing room, Tea, Mown Hay, Cypress, Firewood, Pomander, Clove, and Rose candles are perfect. Moreover, they have the bonus of eliminating any persistent smell of tobacco. In the dining room, fresh notes are better than heavy and heady scents, which might detract from the flavor of the food. On the other hand, orange blossom, vervain, mint, tomato leaf, and generally all types of leaves are welcome guests.

Improvised candles

A scented candle can be improvised by pouring a few drops of perfumed essence into the hot wax of a dish-warmer candle, used as a candle holder. Light the candle, melt the wax (if it is placed in a glass container, do not forget to put some water at the bottom, so that the glass does not heat up in contact with burning metal), and then extinguish the wick. Pour out the perfumed essence.

This procedure can be used for any candle, but you should never apply the essence when the flame is burning.

Flowers and candles

Choose a fairly wide bowl, and pour a small amount of water into it. Stand a small scented candle or dish-warmer candle in it and sprinkle the bowl with rose petals or any other kind of flower.

For end-of-year festivities you can also slip candles between clementines or small apples (such as those you gather from ornamental apple trees), arranged close together—the golden flame emanating from the candles harmonizes beautifully with the orange tones of these winter fruits.

Clementines as night lights

In winter rediscover your childhood pastimes by transforming a string of clementines into so many small night lights, which you can set along on the mantelpiece.

Cut the fruits into halves through the middle (in the same way as you would to squeeze an orange) and carefully remove the flesh while trying to preserve the long central filament, which you use as a wick. Pour some vegetable oil halfway up one half of each fruit.

Light the wick and place the other half over it, as a lid. Do not forget to make a small hole at the top, otherwise the flame will go out. Those who are less skilled with their hands can skip the wick-and-vegetable-oil stage and just place a small dish-warmer candle inside the fruit. As it burns it will light up the clementine and transform it into a veritable fruit of the Hesperides, with a unique fragrance drifting gently through the house.

Perfumed skin

You make me lose my senses, my sister, o bride…

How delicious your love is, more delicious than wine!

And the fragrance of your perfumes, more fragrant than balsam!

Your lips, o bride, distil the virgin honey.

Honey and milk are the language you speak;

And the perfume of your clothes is like the perfume of the Lebanon.

The Song of Songs.

The fashion in perfume is changing. Thus, nard, an aromatic plant inaccurately described as belonging to the Labiate family (like lavender), the Valerianaceae family, or the Gramineae family of plants found in marshy terrains, very precious and considered a treasure in antiquity, has today totally disappeared from general use. But you still find there is a kind of constant of rich scents, such as those that were loved in antiquity and those yet popular in Asia today.

The rose, then musk, and amber, reigned enduringly supreme over these opulent fragrances, worthy of *The Thousand and One Nights*. But in the eighteenth century an inverted trend began to set in. Queen Marie-Antoinette had made light and flowery perfumes fashionable, evoking a natural idyll in the image of her Petit Trianon château at Versailles. Towards the end of the nineteenth century, respectable women (and even other kinds) did not scent themselves, or did so only very little with natural essences of vervain or violet, adored by the empress Eugénie. In *Nana*, Émile Zola perfumes his heroine with this sweet smell. She was so heavily scented with it that it could be

Traditional violet water

1l (1¾pt) 90 proof alcohol
100g (4oz) orris root powder
200g (7oz) benzoin powder

Steep the orris root powder in the alcohol
for a week, then add the benzoin tincture.
Filter, then pour into a bottle.
  As violets are very difficult to distill,
often just their leaves are used; or they
are replaced, as in this case, by orris root
powder, which has an unbeatable,
marvelous scent of violet powder.

detected in every room she occupied, particularly the drawing room: "The afternoon fire died down to reveal glowing embers; it was very warm, with a languid heat, under the curtains and the portières. And in this room, imbued with the intimate life of Nana, where her gloves, a fallen handkerchief, or an open book lay around, she would be found in a state of undress with her scent of violets...."

As for Colette, in recalling her mother Sido in *Claudine's House*, she does not mention real perfume nor even eau de toilette, but writes of a fragrant atmosphere, drifting around this beloved individual in their midst: "My mother's scent was like washed cretonne, the iron heated up over embers of poplar wood, the lemon-scented vervain leaf that she rolled up in her hands or crumpled in her pocket."

Eau de cologne

500ml (16 fl oz) 90 or 70 proof alcohol
6 drops lemon essence
6 drops citron essence
6 drops orange flower essence
6 drops bergamot essence
3 drops rosemary essence
3 drops lavender essence

Blend all the ingredients. Shake well, then filter and pour into a small flask. This recipe, one of the numerous variations on the original eau de cologne recipe, is taken from a perfumery manual dating from the early twentieth century.

You can add to these ingredients 500ml (16 fl oz) orange blossom water and 250ml (8fl oz) rosewater, taking care to mix them with the alcohol before adding the essences. These flower waters provide a little more body and freshness to the cologne.

THE LONG HISTORY OF EAU DE COLOGNE In every beauty manual for women in the Edwardian era there were recipes for scented waters, inspired by the recipe for eau de cologne, which gave the skin a discreet fragrance while respecting proprieties and not arousing the senses unduly. The eau de cologne formula was invented in the late seventeenth century by an Italian, Giovanni Paolo (Jean-Paul) Feminis, who had undoubtedly been captivated by two famous waters during the course of his travels across Europe: one was Queen of Hungary Water, which had a base of citron and rosemary; the other was Aqua di Regina (Queen's Water), whose elements (lemon, citron, bergamot, and neroli) suggested the Hesperides, and which was perfected for Catherine de Médici by the nuns of the Santa Maria di Novella convent in Florence.

Having set up as a perfumer in Cologne, and inspired by these scents, Jean-Paul Feminis created Aqua Mirabilis (Wondrous Water) in 1695, handing down the secret formula to a nephew, Jean-Marie Farina, who rechristened it eau de cologne. Established in Paris in 1808, one of his descendants was to distribute this famous perfume throughout the world. It could count among its users the emperor Napoleon, who was so enamored with this fresh water that he had special 'rolls' made out of it, which he took with him everywhere, pushed into his boots. Thus he could rub himself down with it and drink a few mouthfuls whenever he wished (at this period it was also drunk as an elixir). Since 1862 eau de cologne Extra-Vieille (Extra Old) has belonged to the company, Roger & Gallet, which still distributes it today just as successfully, more than 300 years after its creation!

Perfumed water

1 l (1¾pt) 60 proof alcohol
4 teaspoons bergamot essence
1½ teaspoons lemon essence
½ teaspoon orange essence
1 teaspoon rosemary essence
2 teaspoons Seville orange (bitter orange)
  essence
2 tablespoons orange-flower essence

Blend all the ingredients and shake well.
Pour into a small flask.

Water of a thousand flowers

1 l (1¾pt) 90 proof alcohol
150ml (¼pt) orange blossom water
6g (¼oz) balsam of Peru (or balsam of Tolu)
1 tablespoon bergamot essence
1 teaspoon clove essence
½ teaspoon orange-flower essence
¼ teaspoon thyme essence
2½ teaspoons amber tincture

Mix the alcohol and orange blossom
water, then add the other ingredients to
this liquid. Steep for a week. Filter, then
pour into a small flask. Instead of amber
tincture, the original recipe recommended
musk; this was the best perfume fixative,
but its sale is now prohibited in order to
protect the animal species that produce it.

The original eau de cologne consisted of spirits of wine (brandy), melissa water, and spirit (essence) of rosemary, combined with essences of bergamot, neroli, citron, and lemon, which gave it a highly recognizable, fresh, tangy scent.

It was available in many forms, more or less amber-colored, with flowers and herbs added. At that time this water was a real panacea. It was considered to be a marvellous antidote to all kinds of poisons, and an excellent preservative against contaminated air and the plague. "Those affected would take five spoonfuls of this water in a quart of tepid water and it would draw out the poison easily," a nineteenth-century text, reproduced in *The Modern Perfumery* in 1912, informs us.

The recipes for perfumed waters suggested here are often taken from books intended for perfumers, and although we have reduced their quantities they may seem too sizeable to you. In that case, go to your herbalist to obtain the ingredients and ask him to prepare it, by still dividing up the quantities if necessary. Many of these recipes had to be distilled. As it is unusual to have a still at home, you can make do with these simple steeping processes, although the results are less enduring than waters obtained after distillation. It is possible to replace the alcohol with brandy or vodka, their aromas being more pleasant than that of pure alcohol.

If you are unable to carry out these recipes, you can simply enhance eau de cologne with a vanilla pod, a few peppercorns, or tiny amber pebbles placed in the bottle.

FOR THE ENJOYMENT OF THE SENSES "He smiled. 'Yes, Madam, perfume is essential for seducing a man, for it brings back unconscious recollections that prompt him to act; perfume creates vague confusion in his mind, troubles and agitates him, in reminding him of his pleasures.'" (Guy de Maupassant, *Tales and Short Stories*.) The perfume that thus seduced the lady's man Maupassant, was quite simply vervain, one of the fresh flower fragrances that were so very popular in the late nineteenth century.

A few years later, everything was to change. With the advent of the twentieth century the modern perfumery was born and many of the greatest perfumes, which we still like wearing today, were created before the Second World War.

Nowadays, while many women remain faithful to one single perfume, most like to change, intoxicated by the creations that continue to multiply each year—the spirit of the times is symbolized by the ephemeral. Thus modern women consumers have now come to resemble Andy Warhol, who admitted to a perfume collector's passion in *THE Philosophy of Andy Warhol (From A to B and Back Again)*: "I switch perfumes all the time. If I've been wearing one perfume for three months, I force myself to give it up, even if I still feel like wearing it, so whenever I smell it again it will always remind me of those three months. I never go back to wearing it again; it becomes part of my permanent smell collection."

Practical advice

Like oil, perfume does not tolerate either heat or light. The ideal solution would be to keep it in a cool place, still inside its original packaging.

Although you should avoid mixing perfumes, directly from bottle to bottle, you can combine perfumes on different parts of the body and in this way build up a very personal scent trail. In order not to make any mistakes, however, it is necessary to know the dominant qualities of perfumes (a perfumer will give you good advice): amber-scented, Oriental, spicy, green, powdery, peppery, flowery, fruity, evoking the Hesperides; pure; bergamot and sandalwood.

Which parts of the body should you anoint? Where you can feel your pulse beat: in the hollow of your wrists, behind your ears, behind your knees. And then in other places, too—between your breasts, on your hair, or wherever you want!

Is it better to apply perfume with a spray or with your hand? Purists say that perfume diffuses better when it is sprayed in microscopic droplets on to the skin. But some perfume lovers, such as the great designer Serge Lutens, confess that even if a little more is wasted, they prefer the contact of the perfume in the palm of the hand, to be then dabbed on the body.

The joys of a beauty routine

Madame Facibey waited for the hairdresser in her apartment.... Aware of the time she had lost, and anxious to break free from the melancholy of the past, she stretched her arms out expansively towards the present and immersed herself in a perfumed bath, as if to wash away the gloomy impressions of memory for ever. Louis de Vilmorin, *Julietta*.

Beauty routines and cleanliness have followed very different paths over time. For the Romans, cleanliness and water were self-evident—you took a communal bath (women on one side, men on the other), and you devoted many a long hour to ablutions and beauty treatments. The hammam, frequented by women of the Muslim world, furthermore, inherited its customs from the Roman world.

Until the Church decreed that it was immoral for men and women to appear nude in the public baths, there was nothing unclean about the Middle Ages, contrary to popular belief today: "A town-crier wandered through the streets of thirteenth-century Paris to summon people to the heat of the steam rooms and baths, just so many well-known establishments that numbered 26 in 1292," Georges Vigarello recalls in *The Clean and the Dirty*, a detailed study of body hygiene in the Middle Ages. As a matter of fact, these establishments were more like Roman baths than public baths, which continued to spread in French cities up to the 1950s, before showers and baths were common features in every apartment.

From the fourteenth century, and particularly from the sixteenth and seventeenth centuries, water became the skin's enemy (doctors imagined skin was 'porous'), liable to transmit infections just by contact. As this dangerous liquid was banned, the use of

Angel skin milk

250ml (8fl oz) orange blossom water
8.5g (⅕ oz) benzoin powder

Pour both ingredients into a bottle and shake well.

In the past, this angel skin milk or virginal milk was a mixture intended for washing the face and body. You poured a little over moist linen and rubbed your skin down with it.

It has a benzoin base, which releases a delicious aroma of amber-scented vanilla. At one time it was an indispensable part of a lady's skincare routine, smoothing the skin out and imparting a healthy glow. Today it is still a marvellous product; you add a few drops to your bath water to fragrance and soften it.

Spice lotion

250ml (8fl oz) rosewater (or orange blossom,
    if you prefer)
2 tablespoons vodka
5 drops vanilla tincture
5 drops cinnamon essence
4 cloves

Mix the flower water and vodka. Add the cloves and leave to steep for a week. Filter, then add the vanilla tincture and cinnamon essence. Be careful with cinnamon essence—in its pure form it can irritate the skin. Be careful when handling it, and heed the quantities given. Blend well. Pour into a bottle.

This delicately scented lotion can be used for massaging into both the body and the scalp.

lotions and of toilet vinegars added to linen became more widespread, and above all, scrupulous attention was paid to clothing and underwear, which had to be changed and washed on a daily basis. What lay beneath was of little consequence, as long as the outward appearance and exterior were fragrant. When a bath was still taken, the aim was not one of hygiene but was a purely medical resort.

This attitude was to continue almost up to the mid-nineteenth century, when women were still advised to wash their hair only once a month. When the baroness d'Orchamps recalled her bathroom, in a book dedicated to *Women's Secrets* and dating from the early twentieth century, she devoted long pages to the decoration of the place, to items that should be found there, but accorded only a few lines to the washing routine itself, during which the body is "more or less stripped, out of necessity," but not completely!

Under the Second Empire men flocked to the private Parisian lodging house belonging to La Païva, a famous courtesan. Two of its rooms caused a scandal—the bedroom where a gigantic sculpted bed had pride of place and was the origin of her fortune; and, above all, the vast marble bathroom, with a bathtub as large as a pool, decorated with sculptures and equipped with gold taps inlaid with precious stones. This unseemly luxury, ostentatiously flaunted, was appropriate for a courtesan but not for either the aristocracy or the French upper-middle classes, which were very prudish.

Times have certainly changed since then…. The era when the comtesse de Pange wrote that none of her family had a bath seems distant. To immerse yourself in a perfumed bath and anoint your body with soothing oil or refreshing milk now forms part of our small daily pleasures, which we would be wrong to deny ourselves.

Cucumber lotion

1 cucumber peeled and cut into strips
1 wine glass rose or orange blossom water
½ teaspoon benzoin tincture

Cucumber has been known for its
refreshing and softening properties for
a very long time. You need only to peel
it and blend it to obtain a natural beauty
treatment that is easy to prepare.

    For a more delicate milk, place all the
ingredients in a mixing bowl. Blend until
you obtain a slightly creamy milk. Filter,
then pour into a bottle. This lotion can be
kept for a week, as long as you put it in
the refrigerator. You can use it after
removing make-up or, in summer, to
refresh your face.

Hand lotion

⅓ glycerine
⅓ eau de cologne
⅓ lemon juice

Pour all the ingredients into a flask. Put
a cork in it and shake the lotion before
using it, to homogenize the mixture. This
old recipe, which is easy to prepare,
makes your hands soft and white,
especially after housework. You can keep
it in a bottle, and put it in the kitchen, for
example, next to the soap.

Cleansing milk

1 small jar fresh cream
1 tablespoon rosewater
1 tablespoon glycerine

Blend all the ingredients and then pour into a bottle.

This milk will keep in the refrigerator, but for no longer than a week. It is suitable for your morning skincare routine and leaves the skin soft and fresh. It cannot replace your usual make-up remover, because it is not strong enough to remove traces of mascara; on the other hand, it is very pleasant to use if you do not normally wear heavy make-up.

English-style perfumed vinegar

200g (7oz) acetic acid
15g ($\frac{1}{2}$oz) camphor powder
1 teaspoon clove essence
1 teaspoon benzoin tincture
$\frac{1}{2}$ teaspoon lavender essence
$\frac{1}{2}$ teaspoon cinnamon essence
$\frac{1}{2}$ teaspoon mint essence
$\frac{1}{2}$ teaspoon thyme essence
3 drops petit grain or orange-flower
    essence

Mix all the ingredients, shake well, and then leave them to rest overnight. Filter, then pour into a bottle. This recipe, dating from the nineteenth century, produces a deliciously perfumed vinegar.

COSMETIC VINEGARS Until the early twentieth century toilet vinegars or cosmetic vinegars were an indispensable supplement to the cleansing routine, as much for women as for men.

In the past, rose vinegar was part of every family's first-aid kit for the treatment of chapped skin and chilblains. Steeping vinegar with red roses gives it a superb ruby color and a delicious perfume. This is what Colette had to say about it, when she recalled the times her mother prepared it: "Going further back in time, much further, I remember that in the summer my mother would prepare, and keep in reserve, a bottle of red rose petals infused in strong vinegar for one month, to be used if her children had those open chilblains that were called 'skin chaps' in our home; the mixture was clarified through filter paper." Colette loved the aroma and the taste of this vinegar so much that she had no hesitation in playing the overtired child, so that Sido, her mother, would rub her with it. Secretly, she would lick her skin afterwards to savor the dual pleasure of the acidity of the vinegar and the perfume of the rose.

You can still use toilet vinegars today, because the vinegar (to be used diluted, never pure) is beneficial for the skin as well as the scalp, re-establishing its natural acidity, which is sometimes thrown out of balance owing to excessive use of soaps and shampoos that are too harsh.

You pour a few drops of it into water, to neutralize the limestone. When washing hair it can be used in the last rinse to make the hair shiny; and if you take care to dilute them with water, these strongly aromatic vinegars leave a light perfume in which the characteristic odor of acetic acid does not dominate.

Vanilla-flavored vinegar

250ml (8fl oz) vinegar
15 drops benzoin tincture
25 drops vanilla extract
25 drops amber tincture

Mix all the ingredients, shake well, filter, and pour into a bottle.

Flower vinegar

250ml (8fl oz) vinegar
15g (½oz) orange blossom
15g (½oz) orange peel
15g (½oz) bitter orange (seville) leaves
15g (½oz) rose petals
15g (½oz) camomile
1 glass orange blossom water
1 glass rosewater

Put the vinegar and dry ingredients into a saucepan and heat the mixture until it boils. Pour into a jar. Cork it and leave it to steep for two weeks. Drain the liquid, and press the flowers vigorously. Filter, then add the orange blossom water and the rosewater. Filter again and pour into a bottle.

Orange blossom vinegar

200g (7oz) orange blossom
250ml (8fl oz) vinegar

Leave the flowers to steep in the vinegar for ten days. Filter, then pour into a bottle.
   You can also use lemontree flowers or grapefruit tree flowers—grapefruit blossom retains its scent and leaves a fragrant trail, which is lacking in orange blossom. If you have the opportunity to grow these trees in your garden, use fresh flowers; otherwise you can find dried flowers at your local herbalist.

Rose vinegar

100g (4oz) highly fragrant red rose petals
500ml (16 fl oz) vinegar

Leave the petals to steep in the vinegar for a month. Then filter and collect the petals, pressing them to squeeze out the liquid. Filter again (this is a very simple operation if you use a paper coffee filter) and pour into a tightly corked bottle.

Traditional rose oil

500 ml (16 fl oz) sunflower oil or olive oil
250g (9oz) scented roses (*Rosa centifolia* or
    damask rose)

Pound the rose petals in a mortar. Pour
them into a clay pot and cover them with
oil. Warm them on a low heat for ten
minutes, then tightly seal the pot and
leave to infuse for at least a fortnight.
    Drain the oil, collect the flowers, and
squeeze them between your hands, over
a container, to extract all the liquid.
    Filter a couple of times, then pour into
a dark-colored glass bottle, to protect the
oil from light.
    Orange blossom oil can be prepared in
the same way.
    You can use dried flowers instead of
fresh, but your oil will be less fragrant.

BODY OILS In Egypt, for festivities and receptions, men and women of the court of the Pharaoh were literally streaming with scented oil, because their custom was to decorate their hair with a cone composed of aromatic fat, which the surrounding heat caused to melt down slowly over their shoulders.

In Ancient Greece refined women anointed their bodies with various perfumed oils, which were prepared by adding aromatic plant essences, obtained by distillation, to precious palm oil or to olive oil, which was more widespread.

Each oil corresponded to a part of the body. *The Art of Perfume: The Domestication of Time* teaches us that "palm oil saturated with mint for the arms, chest, and cheeks; marjoram unguent for the hair and eyebrows; and rosewater for the breasts, hips, and stomach" were used.

There was also rose oil, produced by the warm steeping of petals of scented roses from Damascus in Syria, *Rosa centifolia* from Mount Bermion in Macedonia, from Crete, from Rhodes ("island of roses"), or from Cyprus. Today it is very easy to prepare a traditional rose oil whose perfume is in no way inferior to that of the oils of the Ancients. Use it after a bath or a shower, on skin that is still moist, so that the oil glides over it smoothly and is absorbed more efficiently.

The beneficial effects of rassoul

In North Africa they mainly use rassoul, a type of soapy clay, for washing the hair so that it is left particularly soft and shiny. They also add a small amount to bathwater, or massage their skin with it straight from the jar.

Rassoul is scent-free but it must be diluted before use. You can use rosewater or orange blossom water instead, or even perfume the paste with a few drops of essence of clove, rose geranium, or orange flower.

SOAPS The use of soap dates back to antiquity (it was invented by the Gauls), but at that time it was only used to wash linen; for their skin the Romans preferred to anoint themselves from head to toe with oil, which they then rubbed over themselves with a flat, sharpened stone, called a strigil. Soap manufacture developed from the twelfth century in Spain and Italy, then in Marseilles in the fifteenth century. However, it was not until the advent of the nineteenth century, and notably Pasteur's work on microbes, that soap became an ally in the struggle against illness by the champions of modernity—for the first time, teachers instructed their pupils on the need to wash their hands with soap several times a day. Today, with their pale or bright colors and their fragrances, soaps belong as much to the realm of sensory pleasures as they do to the realm of hygiene.

In the United States, there is a veritable craze for homemade soaps. The numerous books published on this subject make it possible to produce soaps exactly as they were made in the past. For beginners it would be better to keep to a simple method and just grate some high-quality soap (as unscented as possible, if you want to perfume it yourself). Then you can melt it in a small amount of liquid (distilled water, milk, aromatic infusions) in a *bain-marie*. When it has completely melted, add all kinds of ingredients: essential oils for perfume, lanolin, glycerine, oats or honey for softness, bran to exfoliate the skin more effectively. When the soapy liquid starts to cool down, you just need to pour it into an oiled mould to give it its shape; or simply, roll the paste between your palms, coated with orris root powder or talc.

Honey and vanilla soap

1 soap
12 drops sweet almond oil
2 tablespoons liquid honey
12 drops vanilla tincture

Grate the soap, then melt it in the bain-marie in a small amount of distilled water. When it has completely dissolved, add the other ingredients and mix gently, by turning over with a wooden spoon. Pour the mixture into a mold and leave to chill in a cool place.

Oriental soap

½ cup rassoul
½ glass water
2 tablespoons rosewater
5 drops rose geranium essence

Gradually pour the rassoul powder into a bowl. Dilute it with water and rosewater to form a slightly liquid but not too runny paste: add some rassoul or water to obtain the required consistency. Shape the soap by pressing the paste between your hands or in a mold.

Coffee soap

1 soap
4 tablespoons rolled oats
4 tablespoons finely ground coffee

This is a surprising idea adapted from a recipe found in an American book: add rolled oats and coffee to the melted soap (household soap for example, or soap flakes). This produces a soap that can be used in the kitchen, as oats are a softening agent and the coffee disperses unpleasant smells of onion, garlic, or fish on your hands.

The secrets of laundresses

A child's attention is held by the most well developed of the senses. Already mine was the sense of smell. My mother had scarcely pronounced the word "washing," and I thought I could smell the sickly-sweet aroma of ashes, scattered over the hemp sheet covering the large wash-tub in the laundry-room, where a bundle of orris root, as white as bones, hung from a nail. Colette, *Journal Against the Grain*.

It is said that Louis XIV required his washerwomen to wash his underwear with a washing powder in which the powerful aromas of cloves, nutmeg, musk, neroli (orange flower), and jasmine were very much in evidence.

This custom of washing linen and simultaneously perfuming it has not been abandoned in our contemporary world—all washing powders are scented (with varying degrees of success), and for a long time softeners have aimed to conquer our noses.

Moreover, in Grasse, home of perfumes since the eighteenth century, the primary purpose of essences is no longer just for making perfumes—with the food industry, the washing-powder industry is the main buyer of natural or synthetic essences.

If you wish, you can still savor the experience of linen washed in the traditional way by using a biological powder and adding a few orris roots to it, to give the linen a scent of violets, as our forefathers commonly did. In England, to perfume the water for washing laundry, elecampane root or sweet-flag root "a kind of scented reed whose perfume reminds you of cinnamon" were also valued. You can find these roots at any herbalist; it is best to keep them for hand-washing small items of clothing.

Past and current ideas

You can use scented roots such as orris root or elecampane root to perfume the water in which you wash your linen. You just need to take the precaution of wrapping them up in a handkerchief or a small cotton square, knotted like a bundle, so that the elements do not disperse and block the pipework.

For delicate hand-washing, use the zest of a lemon in the final rinse, wrapped up in a handkerchief. This brings out the whiteness of the linen, as well as softening and perfuming it.

If you are not partial to the perfume of industrial washing powders, which is often overwhelming, replace them occasionally with household soap shavings or flakes. These can be used perfectly well in a washing machine, as long as you do not exceed two handfuls per wash, which is the amount required. Any more than this and the soap produces too much foam. Always finish with a vinegar rinse.

To prepare a homemade softener, pour the contents of a packet of bicarbonate of soda into a small jar. Add a few drops of your favorite essential oil. Blend well and tightly seal the jar. Before you do your washing, put a tablespoon of this mixture into the rinsing-agent compartment.

If you live in an area where the tapwater is extremely hard, adopt the habit of pouring a glass of spirit vinegar into the rinsing-agent compartment. This will eliminate all traces of soap.

You can also use spirit vinegar perfumed with a few drops of essential oil (lavender, rosemary, ylang ylang, vetiver) for all your rinses. This is far kinder to the skin than an industrial softener and enables you to perfume your linen with the fragrance of your choice.

Lavender starch

125g (4½oz) starch in powder or crystal form
2 pinches of table salt
3l (5¼pt) cold water
20 drops lavender essence

In a small basin gradually dilute the starch and table salt in cold water (salt prevents the starch from sticking to a hot iron), while mixing well so that there are no lumps.

Add the lavender essence. Mix well. Soak the linen in the starch water so that it is completely saturated. Then wring it out thoroughly, without rinsing, and iron it when it is still fairly damp.

FLOWER WATERS FOR LINEN There are now all kinds of delicately perfumed flower waters for ironing purposes: lavender, orange blossom water, lime blossom water. But before you use them you should look at your iron's directions for use; some do not tolerate these products. If this is the case, spray the water directly on to your laundry before you iron. You can also mix these perfumed waters with starch, sold in an atomizer. Use two-thirds starch to one-third perfumed water. Starch works wonders on fine linen, especially flax linen, which it prevents from creasing unduly, and on white shirts, to which it lends firmness. You can buy starch in an aerosol or a spray, but it is not difficult to prepare yourself. You can still find starch in the form of powder in some traditional hardware shops, and as an alternative rice water is an excellent natural starch.

Sachet of cloves

Simply fill a sachet with cloves, using a few drops of benzoin essence as a perfume fixative. You can add dried orange peel to it, cut into small pieces, as its scent harmonizes beautifully with the aroma of the cloves. Cloves are an excellent natural moth repellent. To revive the perfume, you just need to rub the sachet between your fingers.

Moth-repellent sachets

There are many recipes for this. Here are two possible variations.

Mix dried leaves of lavender, lemonbalm, and wormwood, in equal parts. To give a more pleasant scent, you can add dried lemon rind, cut into pieces, and a few drops of bergamot essence. Fill a sachet with the mixture and hang it in a wardrobe or mix dried leaves of vervain, lavender, scented pelargonium, and peppermint, in equal parts.

SCENTING LINEN IN THE TRADITIONAL WAY In the past, once it was washed, dried in the open air, and ironed, linen was put away in wardrobes and chests of drawers, into which were always put sachets or bunches of lavender, or any other aromatic plant, traditionally reserved for wardrobes. They perfumed the linen while repelling flies, mites, and other destructive insects.

Since Roman antiquity lavender has been associated with bathwater (in Latin, 'to wash' and 'lavender'—*lavare* and *lavandula*—have the same root) and air purity. Hence, massive lavender pyres were burnt during epidemics, or smaller pyres at funerals. We undoubtedly owe the practice of placing lavender among linen to these ancient rites, as its perfume expresses both cleanliness and hygiene. In Provence, the custom of using bunches of lavender for decoration and for scenting the interior of wardrobes, cupboards, and drawers is so deeply rooted that even today little girls are taught how to make them. Children's fingers become rapidly skillful in folding the stems in bloom back on themselves, so as to form a kind of scented 'cage' around which delicate satin ribbons are woven, passing one by one between the sprigs.

On Réunion, in Madagascar and in the Comoros Islands, vetiver roots are popular, bound into small bundles or woven in the shape of a fan, which have the power to protect against insects, while spreading a delectable aroma (to revive the scent, you just need to moisten the vetiver lightly).

In Kashmir weavers of long ago sent their precious shawls to Europe, protected by patchouli leaves, which imbued them with a wonderful earthy scent, woody, and moist.

Nowadays in India saris, precious clothes, and shawls, which, together with her jewels represent the entire fortune of a bride, are meticulously stored in chests giving off a strong smell of camphor. This product has always been used in China as well. Still today, when you buy an Indian shawl or a pullover made of Chinese cashmere you come upon the unmistakable aroma, with which they are imbued over long months. Camphor, which is undoubtedly the most powerful natural moth repellent, is extracted from the camphor-tree, an exotic tree resembling the laurel. It releases a very strong and individual aroma (close to Chinese tiger balm, used for massages) but it is much more pleasant than mothballs, a chemical product derived from petrol that has been the enduring cause of reeking wardrobes and clothes since the late nineteenth century.

In Asia a lot of cedar wood and thuya wood is also used to make chests in which linen and clothes are put away. The virtues of the cedar are known throughout the world and in America, not so long ago, women settlers would use cedar shavings rather than European lavender. At traditional herbalists you can find dried leaves of patchouli (for those who like its very individual fragrance it is an ideal moth repellent), cedar or sandalwood shavings, and camphor as powder or crystals.

Rose and lavender sachet

125g (4½oz) rosebuds
100g (4oz) lavender seeds
5 cloves
5 drops benzoin tincture
1 muslin or cotton sachet

Place the rosebuds, lavender, and cloves
in the bowl of a mincer and turn on the
appliance for a few seconds, until they
are reduced to a fairly coarse powder.
Add the benzoin as a perfume fixative.
Blend well. Spoon this scented powder
into the sachet.

For a more attractive finish you can
decorate the sachet with a pattern (see
photograph above) and tie it with ribbon.

Traditional scented sachet

4 parts scented rose petals
3 parts dried carnation petals
2 parts orris root powder
2 parts ground coriander seeds
1 part sweet-flag root cut into small pieces
1 part benzoin powder
1 muslin or cotton sachet

Blend all the ingredients. Put them into a
sachet, to hang in a closet or cabinet.

Sachet from the South of France

1 part lavender
1 part thyme
1 part marjoram
1 part santolina
1 part rosemary
1 part strawflower (everlasting flower) leaves
    (*Helichrysum*)
1 muslin or cotton sachet

Blend the dried plants and fill your sachet.

Aromatic sachet

100g (4oz) lavender
50g (2oz) tansy
25g (1oz) strawflower (*Helichrysum*)
25g (1oz) vervain
1 muslin or cotton sachet

Blend the dried plants and fill your sachet.

Amber sachet

Amber leaves stain if they are in direct contact with the item they are going to perfume. To make this sachet, designed for clothes, you should combine two kinds of fabric: a thin fabric for the first envelope and a thicker one to protect the clothes from the amber.

Fold the two strips of fabric, one on top of the other, in two to form a sachet. With the thicker fabric on the inside, sew up the sides, then turn inside out so that the thicker fabric is on the outside. Then slip fossil-resin amber pebbles inside (about 25g (1oz) for a small sachet).

PERFUMING LEATHER SHOES My grandmother, refined right down to the tips of her

court shoes, used to soak a piece of flannel in sandalwood essence and daub the leather

interiors of all her shoes with it. So when she took her shoes off she left a mysterious

trail behind her that evoked the forests of India. Sandalwood has become an extremely

precious material as felling the trees from which the essence is extracted is prohibited;

but there are still many other ways to make leather shoes smell sweet. Placed right

inside the shoe, a mixture of dried peppermint and sage reduced to powder, with a

pinch of alum in powder form added, will be very beneficial in other respects, especially

in sports shoes, as sage and alum reduce perspiration considerably.

Sachets for leather shoes

Small balls of clay used to improve
houseplant compost or for hydroponics
(cultivation of plants without soil, in water
containing dissolved nutrients) are both
very light and porous. Soak them for
several days in an essential oil, or an oil
used for burning; the fragrance will last
a long time. Wrap them in a small cloth
sachet, to slip into your shoes.

Amber

Amber is ideal for giving a pleasant fragrance to leather shoes, particularly women's shoes. We are not talking about mythical ambergris, the precious substance found floating on sea foam and whose source remained a mystery for a long time. (Now we know that it results from secretions from sperm whales whose intestines are irritated by colossal ingestion of squid.) The type we suggest using is fossil-resin amber, which takes the form of small pebbles; its pleasant, appealing aroma, which has a strong, sweet note of vanilla, can give an enduring fragrance to fabrics, leather, and even jewelry. It can be found in Oriental grocery stores that sell North African products, and in the souks of Morocco or Tunisia.

In the middle of the night

I rested my cheeks tenderly against the beautiful cheeks of the pillow, which, plump

and fresh, are like the cheeks of our childhood. Marcel Proust, *Swann's Love*.

Sleep often calls for a ritual, sometimes inherited from childhood, or quite simply

intended to help those who have difficulty in falling asleep. To make the process easier,

here are a few little ideas that will fill the night with fragrance and invite sleepers into

a happy dreamland. Slip on a very clean nightdress perfumed with your favourite eau de

toilette. Feel free to substitute a T-shirt, pyjamas, or even nothing at all, following the

example of Marilyn Monroe who used to sleep 'dressed' in Chanel No. 5! Climb into

a bed whose sheets have just been changed that very day, and savor the feel of freshly

ironed cotton or linen, still somewhat stiff, and giving off a light perfume of washing

powder, lavender, or soap.

Just before you go to bed, fragrance your pillow with a scented blend that will

promote calm and relaxation; for example, a dash of orange blossom or lime blossom

water, a few drops of bergamot or orange flower essence.

Slip a cover of thin cotton or muslin sachet filled with scented plants into your

pillow or eiderdown, to encourage fragrant dreams. Vervain, lavender, every variety

of mint, camomile, hops, and scented asperula (Rubiaceae) are particularly beneficial.

For sheer visual and olfactory pleasure, place a sprig of vervain, a passionflower with

its exquisite aroma, a rose or a perfumed carnation on the half-open sheet or the pillow.

You could also put them in a glass or jug of water on the bedside table just before you

fall asleep, so that you will find them still fresh the next morning.

Scented water for pillows

250ml (8fl oz) orange blossom water
100ml (3fl oz) 70 proof alcohol
10 drops bergamot essence
5 drops mandarin essence
5 drops ylang-ylang essence
3 drops jasmine essence
3 drops sandalwood essence

Mix the flower water and alcohol, and then add the essences. Mix and filter. Pour into an atomizer and spray this water over your pillow in the evening, before going to sleep.

For the lazier among us, there is also a delicious scented water for pillows available at Fragonard.

Mouthwatering fragrances

But when nothing survives from the ancient past…. Aroma and flavors persist for a long time to come…. To carry unflinchingly, on their almost intangible droplet, the vast edifice of remembrance. Marcel Proust, *Swann's Way*.

The kitchen is a magical place where an unsettling alchemy occurs, contributing to the awakening of the senses. We admire the colors of fruits and vegetables; we dip our hands into flour; we cut food into tiny pieces; we snip herbs finely; we inhale aromas and fragrances; and we taste a thousand dishes, which are transformed under our very eyes by sizzling or melting gently over the heat.

Above all, the kitchen is a place where memories are stored, intermingled with sweet and salty aromas. These aromas make your mouth water, whether they are of 'an old favorite' such as evening soup simmering gently on the stove; a green and peppery symphony of leeks and onions, sweetened with carrots and potatoes; or are of faraway places: subtle meat or vegetable stews from Asia, fine Indian curries. Not to mention, of course, toasted bread spread with butter, and morning coffee; hot chocolate or afternoon tea; summer jams; the first clementines of winter; freshly picked herbs; spices from the ends of the earth. All these fragrances paint the most vivid of pictures, one that communes with all the senses.

Useful plants

The perfume of certain aromatic plants is repellent to pests. The virtues of basil and scented geraniums against flies are well known. You just need to put some in pots on your windowsills to make undesirable insects take flight.

But did you know that ants hate the pungent smell of tomato leaves, as well as the scent of lavender? Put some posies in places they frequent, or thin out the leaves and scatter them directly on their path. This method does take longer to have an effect than applying a chemical insecticide, but it is much less dangerous and more fragrant.

In a country house that is unoccupied during the winter months, hang in each room and in the larders, bouquets of wild mint cut in the fields (it has a stronger aroma than domesticated mint), lime blossom, and wild fennel—their smell is repellent to rats.

Adopt the habit of pouring essence of thyme into your sink regularly. It disinfects and purifies the atmosphere.

GOOD-QUALITY HERBS In France it is difficult to cook without aromatic herbs. The French even have a Holy Trinity: parsley (the very curly-leaved variety that the butcher or fishmonger still kindly offers, although the flat-leaved variety is best); thyme, whose very individual aroma seems to contain the whole of the South of France; and bay-leaf, which gives the bouquet-garni all its flavor. But many others are used to enhance the flavor of dishes: basil for tomatoes; aniseed-flavored fennel for fish and gherkin preserves; rosemary for all grilled or roasted meats, the 'satyr herb' (savory) to make dried beans more digestible; tarragon for salads and white meats; peppermint for red strawberries and green peas; cream of sage for pork. And there are still more that come from distant countries, such as citronella and purple basil; the coriander or *kesbor* of Moroccan meat or vegetable stews; and lime leaves, an essential ingredient for Thai or Vietnamese cuisine.

All these good-quality herbs will perhaps replace those that have disappeared from our gourmet horizon. Nowadays who eats orache, pimpernel, parsley-piert, stag's-horn fern, tansy, cordiole, or young balsam—included by Alexandre Dumas among the everyday herbs intended to season delicacies and salads? And their scents, which conjure up images of travel, of escape to distant shores, will fill our kitchen with fragrance just as those wild herbs scented the dishes of yesteryear.

Ideas for the kitchen

The kitchen, too, has a right to be decorated with bouquets: you can find a place for mint, flowering thyme, sage, and green and purple basils in glasses or small jars. Depending on the season, you can add nasturtiums (you can remove a few flowers from these to put into a salad), wild pinks, small roses, or chive flowers with their large mauve pompoms, which give off a very pleasant aroma of onions.

To preserve fresh herbs longer, wash them meticulously; wrap them in moist, kitchen towel, and then in a tea towel. You can also put them in a glass containing a small amount of water (the end of the stems should soak in the water, but not the leaves, which will rot). If you do this, change the water every day.

If you have enough space in your kitchen, devote a small area to drying aromatic herbs: thyme, bay, sage, rosemary, savory, lemonbalm. If you are concerned that they will shed their leaves, you can also wrap them in paper sachets, but they will be much less decorative.

Traditionally a bouquet-garni consists of bay-leaf, thyme, and parsley. For ragouts and stews you can add celery and leeks. And if you like herbs, there is nothing to stop you adding marjoram, sage, fennel (for lightly boiled fish), rosemary, and even basil. In Spain the bouquet-garni is wrapped up in a net of kitchen twine, which makes it easier to remove at the end of cooking; while in Anglo-Saxon countries a little muslin sachet is preferred, in which all the ingredients are neatly confined.

You can make crowns or decorative designs with rosemary and bay (less easily with sage). You just wind the herbs round a rigid but fairly pliable piece of string so that you can give them the required shape. The branches are fixed here and there with green metal wire, curved like a hairpin. You can in this way fashion a crown, a heart or letters of the alphabet to hang on a wall or over a door.

ON THE SPICE ROAD The earth is a jewel case; the herbarium is a perfume burner;

cinnamon, mace, nutmeg, ginger, opium, hashish, rose oil, betel nut, capsicum, date

sugar, Himalayan tea, aloes, saffron, indigo from Salem and Madras: does all this not

resemble the spice mountain of which Solomon spoke? Théophile Gautier wondered

in *The Orient*.

   With spices, the dreams, perfumes, and colors of distant countries enter the

kitchen. The history of spices is a lengthy epic, peppered with voyages of long duration,

merciless wars fought on land and on the oceans; a history confined forever inside a box

or a flask filled with powerful scents and aromas. By breathing in cinnamon, cloves, or

nutmeg, you escape beyond the seas, towards the trading posts of India, Java, Sumatra,

or the Moluccas.

Garam masala

4 tablespoons cardamom
4 tablespoons cumin
4 tablespoons black pepper
4 tablespoons cloves
4 tablespoons cinnamon
4 tablespoons turmeric
4 tablespoons grated nutmeg

Split the cardamom cloves and remove the small brown grains with a knife.

Put all the spices in a non-stick frying pan and cook on a low heat for five minutes. Let it cool, then put this blend of fried spices through a coffee grinder, to obtain a highly scented powder that you put into a tightly sealed jar.

Store your mixture in a dark place. It will keep for about six months. You need about two spoonfuls for four servings of meat, vegetables, or fish.

Spice bread is one of these confections with exotic perfumes. Was its precursor the *melitounta* of Ancient Greece, a bread with a sesame, spices, and honey base; or was it the *mi-kong*, a bread cooked in the oven, made from wheat flour, spices, and honey, which has been made in China since the tenth century? Whatever the case, two French cities claim to have created it: Dijon and Rheims have entertained gourmets with its delights since the Middle Ages. Curiously, you find precious few spices in the classic recipe, where aniseed dominates, but you can add cinnamon, nutmeg, and cloves, according to taste. Another symbolic preparation of the spice cuisine, the garam masala, an Indian seasoning, is used to make numerous curries. Contrary to popular belief, the word 'curry' does not refer to a spice but to a dish with sauce, something like stew (in the Tamil language, *kahri* means 'sauce'), seasoned with a large number of spices, among which you will nearly always find golden, perfume-free turmeric, giving it its characteristic color; and also cumin, ground coriander, and cardamom, which give these dishes an incomparable fragrance, offsetting the formidable force of chili, which is widely used.

In India curry is also a plant of the Rutaceae family, whose leaves recall our bay-leaf. They are tossed into hot oil at the start of preparing a dish, so that they release their aroma.

Spice bread

250g (9oz) flour
10g (¼oz) baking powder
2 eggs
100ml (3fl oz) milk
225g (8oz) honey
1 pinch ground cinnamon
1 pinch grated nutmeg
1 pinch green anise or star anise powder
1 knob butter

Mix the flour (you can mix wheat flour with rye flour in equal parts) and the baking powder in a terrine and make a well in it. Break the eggs into the terrine, then add the milk and spices, then the honey that you will have melted gently. Mix all the ingredients with a whisk, until you obtain a smooth, lump-free paste.

Pour the paste into a loaf tin greased with butter and cook in a moderate oven (200°C/400°F/gas mark 6) for one hour.

This spice bread is better if you wait at least 24 hours before eating. To keep it fresh, wrap it in plastic wrap, which will make it even softer.

Truffle eggs

The fragrance of truffles is so powerful that you need only seal some in a jar with some eggs for the eggs to be imbued with their heavenly aroma.

Then you can eat the eggs boiled or scrambled, with fingers of bread sliced from a delicious loaf, and spread with a thin layer of salted butter.

Colette's simple truffles

In "The Fire under the Embers" in *Prisons and Paradise* Colette gives us a truffle recipe that is very easy to make: "As it was too expensive for us, in winter the Périgord truffle gave way to the Puisaye truffle, which is grey and almost insipid, and whose perfume misleads the uninformed. But grey or black, wrap the scrubbed truffle in an oiled paper wrapper, then slip it in the front of the fire, in a small mound of very hot ash. Lift off tiny embers from the top of the minute burial mound—the idea is that, with the aid of a nimble hand, half an hour later you will unearth truffles, to be eaten with a sprinkling of salt."

THE BLACK PERFUME OF THE SOIL It is hard to evoke fragrances associated with cooking without mentioning the truffle, this mysterious tuber with its powerful, sensual, and enchanting aroma, almost animal-like, which grows only in certain types of soil. A luxury dish, the truffle was already valued in Ancient Rome. In her book *A Natural and Moral History of Food*, Maguelonne Toussaint-Samat, in this regard, quotes this exclamation by a Latin poet, Alledius: "Oh! Libyan, keep your wheat for yourself, unyoke your oxen, but send us your truffles!"

A strange mushroom born of an irritant symbiosis with the truffle-producing oak, certain hazel trees or even Austrian pines, the truffle christened by Brillat-Savarin 'the black diamond of cooking' is a veritable Attila that devastates any surrounding soil in which it decides to grow. To detect it, sows (more docile and gentle than boars) are brought in or dogs trained from a very young age to sniff from a great distance the fragrant treasure, which is then extracted from its layer of soil. When they are sold, truffles, like precious stones, are sometimes concealed, nestling in a scruffy paper wrapping or even in a sock. Nobody needs to catch sight of them to know they are there, as they fill the whole market with their extraordinary aroma. They are revealed only at the moment of sale, when the seller presents the offering in his open left hand, right under the nose of the buyer. It is a very unusual sale, evoked by Maguelonne Toussaint-Samat: "prices are exchanged like passwords. It is either agreed or not agreed. By midday everything is sold; the truffles have disappeared. All that remains is an exquisite fragrance fading away into the streets of the town."

Blackberry jam

1kg (2lb) blackberries
1kg (2lb) granulated sugar
Juice of one lemon

Tip the washed blackberries, with
their stalks removed, into a salad bowl.
Sprinkle them with sugar and steep them
overnight.

The next day, pour this preparation into
a copper pan. Add the juice of the lemon
and heat. Boil for five minutes. Pass
through a sieve to separate the fruits from
the syrup, then return the syrup to the boil
for a further five minutes.

Repeat this procedure three times
(cooked in this way, the fruits will remain
whole). After cooking, put into jars. Close
the jars immediately and turn them upside
down a few times to expel any air.

A NICHE FOR JAMS "The flavor and fragrance of jams often stick to memories of
childhood, recollections of greed associated with minor domestic plundering, with the
attraction of forbidden fruit, with the melting pleasure of reward, with exquisite displays
of gluttony," Nicole Benoît-Lapierre reflects in *Fragrances: The Essence of a Sense*. Like
her, who can say they have no childhood memories of jams? Behind our holiday home a
thorny, insurmountable bush sprawled. At Easter it was adorned with flowers similar to
small dog-roses, of a pink color that was almost mauve. When summer came it was the
season for berries: at first crimson and appetizing but inedible, they then changed color
to ink-black. I had no hesitation in braving the thousand dreadful thorns of the
bramble bush to grasp these wild, delicious treasures. We filled salad bowls to the brim
with them, proudly bearing them back to the kitchen.

Our quest was rewarded first by the fragrance escaping from the pan, then by the right

we had acquired to scrape the inside surface clean with a wooden spoon, meticulously

licked. The delicious berries, a good part of which we had sacrificed on our way home,

were transformed into darkly translucent jellies and into jams whose tiny seeds

crunched under your teeth, and which were kept for the winter months because they

were 'good for the throat.'

Although the sparkling copper pan is a classic utensil imprinted on the memory,

there is no need for one to prepare a batch of jars for the whole year. The arrival of

exquisite mirabelle plums, raspberries, and strawberries in the markets can justify the

preparation of a few jars, which will be quickly ready, especially if you cook your jams

in a microwave.

Perfuming jams

Borrowed from *Grand Dictionary of Cooking* by Alexandre Dumas, here are two surprising ideas to give an unusual, original flavor to apple or quince jelly. After cooking just add three drops (no more) of rose essence or orange flower essence and cook for a few seconds, until the alcohol has evaporated.

An English custom is to add a rose-scented, lemon-scented, or mint-scented pelargonium leaf to these jellies; the jagged silhouette of the leaf seen through the perfumed jelly is prettily decorative.

Tea, coffee, and chocolate

On Sunday mornings when I was eight years of age, sleeping in the giant room that was heated by a single-stove Godin, I was awakened by the warm, reassuring aroma of bread that Maman Flore had begun to knead the day before. It would be accompanied by thick vanilla chocolate, perfumed with an unfathomable suggestion of lemon.

Ina Césaire, *Mother Flore—Or No. 29.*

Why unite these three drinks in a single chapter? Perhaps because they are often grouped together on the menus of cafés and tea rooms. Perhaps also because they stand next to one another on the kitchen shelves, not far from the sugar, honey, and jams; and because, in addition, they appeared practically simultaneously on our Western tables, after great travelers had discovered their dazzling aromas for our benefit.

Sometimes fragrant additives further enhance their flavor. Tea flirts with tangy bergamot. Coffee is pepped up with cardamom, as in Asia. And chocolate becomes smoother with vanilla and cinnamon (in the seventeenth century people had no qualms about scenting it with real amber). If all three are often combined, each tells its own story throughout a history filled with legends, myths, and adventures, and each drink is the subject of very specific rites and customs.

Cake made with green tea
by Mariage-Frères

5 eggs
1 pinch salt
50g (2oz) granulated sugar
250g (9oz) butter + 1 piece for the pan
200g icing sugar
225g (8oz) flour
1 packet yeast
15g (½oz) green tea powder (macha;
    see page 136)

Separate the whites of the eggs from the yolks. Beat the egg whites until stiff, mix with a pinch of salt, then add the granulated sugar.

In a bowl work the softened butter into the icing sugar, until the mixture turns white and forms a cream. Add and mix in the egg yolks one by one.

Sprinkle the flour mixed with the yeast into the bowl, while stirring slowly until the cream is adequately homogenized. Add the green tea powder.

Finally, blend the whipped-up whites very carefully, lifting the mixture slowly, so that they do not collapse.

Pour the mixture into a greased (with butter) cake pan and put in the oven at 220°C/425°F/gas mark 7 for ten minutes; then lower the heat to 200°C/400°F/gas mark 6 and cook for a further 30 minutes.

Mariage-Frères is a specialty tea store in Paris, but green tea is available in the U.S. at Williams-Sonoma.

THE TEA OF SERENITY Tea is the most widespread beverage in the world, and was available long before coffee, alcohol, or carbonated drinks. But whether teas are green, yellow, black, or red, we have become accustomed to enjoying them without concerning ourselves very much with their origin. The drink of immortality, tea does, however, have its rules and conventions, which are observed in genuine tea rooms, where only authentic teas with rare and delicate flavors are served; there is no comparison with the beverages we habitually enjoy elsewhere. Tea experts know how to distinguish them, just as wine connoisseurs know how to identify wines.

In *The Time of Tea*, Dominique Pasqualini, quoting Sheng Fu (*Six Stories as the Changeable Days Drift By*), tells the story of flower-based teas, predecessor of flavored teas: "In summer, when the lotus started to blossom, Yun wrapped a few tea leaves in a small gauze sachet, which in the evening she placed in a lotus corolla before the flower closed up; and in the morning, as soon as the lotus opened up again, she retrieved the sachet; we then made some tea with spring water, whose fragrance was particularly subtle." Fu also noted that in the past tea was infused with jasmine, osmanthus (a small flower with a perfume similar to ripe apricots), rose, wild rose, orchid, orange blossom, magnolia, plum tree blossom, and lotus flower.

Although despised by purists and connoisseurs, teas flavored and perfumed with flowers or fruits are nevertheless so visually beautiful, glistening with the vivid colors of petals or leaves, that sometimes you might like to use them for unusual potpourris, with a very sophisticated scent. On the other hand, it would be best to avoid teas infused with essences that are not always natural—essences that conjure a cake shop, a sweet shop, or even a perfumery.

The art of tea making

For tea to release the full riches of its aroma, it is important to observe a certain degree of ceremony.

The teapot (preferably earthenware; the best come from China) must be warmed before you add the leaves. Pour a few drops of boiling water over the leaves, then strain it away to remove tannins and residues. Finally, pour boiling water into the pot for the third time, then let the leaves infuse for a few minutes, before you can enjoy the fragrant, russet-colored brew.

Green-tea powder

Japanese macha or jade moss is a
powdered green tea used for the tea
ceremony. During this Zen ritual boiling
water and the emerald-green powder are
slowly beaten with a bamboo whisk in a
large bowl (the *chasen*), until a frothy, light
consistency is obtained, with a fairly acrid
and bitter flavor.

Flavored tea

This is a subtle way of flavoring a fairly
bland tea: simply stir it with a cinnamon
stick as a spoon.

Lessons in coffee making

Like connoisseurs, choose coffee beans rather than instant coffee, and grind them at the last moment to preserve all the aromas released from delicious mocha.

When you grind the beans, you can add a pinch of table salt, which will strengthen the flavor.

Serve bitter, black chocolate with the coffee—it is an ideal combination.

Mazagran

150ml (¼pt) ground coffee
1.5l (2½ pt) water
75g (3oz) sugar
50ml (2fl oz) cognac, armagnac, liqueur brandy or another spirit

Prepare the coffee and let it cool down. When you serve it, dilute it with a small amount of water, sugar it to taste, and add the spirit.

This recipe dates from the nineteenth century. Mazagran is a town in Algeria where the French won a battle during the colonization of this country. It is a cold drink, to be served as a liqueur or brandy in a tall, stemmed glass (like an absinthe glass) or in a porcelain goblet.

COFFEE FROM ARABIA FELIX "Before the invention of coffee by an elderly alchemist in Arabia, the world was without fragrance. There had to be great aridity without flowers in order for the flower of flowers, with its delicate voluted columns to grow.... After drinking coffee, port is a stimulating complement." Salah Stétié.

What would our mornings be like without the aroma of coffee gradually permeating the house, this fragrance that evokes the bitterness and darkness of so aromatic a drink? The history of coffee takes us back to Yemen in the early eighteenth century. In 1712 a delegation from France reached al-Mukhà (Mukalla), a port in Yemen. The ambassadors stayed in the country for a few weeks and were invited to meet the king. They were particularly captivated by the Yemeni custom of drinking coffee—so much so that the king's envoy, La Roque wrote *Memorandum Concerning the Coffee Shrub and Fruit*. He described how the Yemeni drank coffee prepared with beans "as in the Levant" (what we today call Turkish coffee), and as people were already drinking it in France at that time. But he was interested above all in a brew with a base of coffee-bean skins, poetically called "the sultana's coffee," and described the recipe thus: "You take the skin from fully ripe coffee beans, break it up and put it into a small pan or terrine over a charcoal fire, turning continuously so that it does not roast like coffee, but only enough to brown it slightly. At the same time, you boil some water in a coffeepot, and when the skin is ready you throw it in with at least a quarter of the fine membrane, boiling the mixture like ordinary coffee..." The 'sultana's coffee' is still drunk in Yemen, and is known today as *qishr* (skin). It is served on a tray with a perfume burner, directed towards the guest's face so that the incense honors him or her with its scent.

Morning pleasures

For some people the pleasure of daybreak
stems from the aroma of freshly made
coffee, or that of toasted bread drifting
beyond the confines of the kitchen as
far as the bedroom. More effective than
an alarm clock, these aromas instantly
announce that night has passed and
a new day is beginning.

Traditional hot chocolate

50g (2oz) dark chocolate
200ml (7fl oz) whole milk
60g (2½oz) butter
10g (¼oz) sugar
1 pinch salt
1 pinch cinnamon or cocoa

This is a really thick creamy chocolate,
flavored to taste, in which you can dunk
a piece of brioche (a light, sweet, bread)
or a madeleine (small sponge cake) that
melts in the mouth.

Break the chocolate into pieces and
mix it with the milk, butter, sugar, and salt
in a saucepan. Bring to a boil, then cook
on a low heat for five minutes. Add the
cinnamon or cocoa and beat with a whisk
until the liquid has a smooth, creamy
consistency, before pouring it into a jug
or a mug.

Sorbet with flavored cocoa

500ml (16fl oz) water
150g (5oz) sugar
50g (2oz) glucose
35g (1¼ oz) best-quality cocoa
sprig of calamint or garden mint

Pour the water, sugar, glucose (glucose
has an advantage over sugar in that it
does not crystallize so readily; if you
cannot find it, replace it with more sugar),
and cocoa in a saucepan. Bring to a boil
and heat for three minutes. Remove from
the heat, immerse the fresh mint leaves
in the cocoa-flavored syrup, and leave
to steep for ten minutes. Strain the liquid,
pour into an ice-cream maker and put
in the freezer to set.

This recipe is taken from *Cookery
Notebook* by Michel Bras. Having settled
in the plateau of Aubrac (in the Auvergne
region), Bras combines cocoa with
calamint (*Calamintha grandiflora*); this
is a wild herb of the region, belonging
to the same family as savory; it releases
a complex aroma, which is powerful and
like menthol. He serves this sorbet with a
liqueur called 'thé d'Aubrac' (the popular
name for calamint), a sweet brandy in
which scented leaves have been steeped.

THE CHOCOLATE OF THE GODS When the Spaniard Hernán Cortés and his army

arrived in Mexico in 1520, they discovered a syrupy drink at the residence of the Aztec

emperor, Montezuma. It had a base of roasted, ground coffee beans, supplemented

with pepper, chili, musk, cornflour, and honey: a heavenly beverage the people called

'tchocoatl.' Cortés took back to Spain like a treasure this 'tchocoatl' that Quetzalcoatl,

the plumed serpent god, had given to mere mortals. With its pepper, chili, and musk

removed, sweetened by sugar, amber, and vanilla, and sometimes enhanced by

cinnamon and cream, then rechristened 'chocolate' it would go on to captivate

Europeans. For a long time it was considered a luxury commodity because it was very

heavily taxed. Despite that, its full-bodied flavor and its intense, almost creamy aroma,

rapidly made it an essential commodity.

Select glossary of scents / **145**

A short, nonexhaustive guide to useful plants and products for making recipes, or for filling your home with fragrance.

Amber-fossil resin

Star anise

Absinthe

Used since the most ancient times, this herb is sometimes known as the 'sacred herb.' It appeared among the medicinal herbs grown in cloisters. Its ash-grey, serrated leaves release a strong, bitter scent, which is a little like wormwood. Use it in small bouquets, or in potpourris with a green-scented theme.

Amber-fossil resin

Made up of various elements with pleasant Oriental scents, suggesting vanilla, this amber is highly valued in the Middle East. It is sold in the form of largely translucent, resinous pebbles, to add to scented waters, toilet vinegars, potpourris, and sachets. It has no connection with the ambergris used by perfume makers, which is a very rare and precious scented substance released by sperm whales, and is collected in the form of 'stones' along certain seashores.

Angelica

Its roots, cut into small pieces, can be used to perfume washing water or to make a scented sachet. Its fragrance is very subtle, with a hint of aniseed.

Basil

No Mediterranean cuisine would be complete without this plant, whose leaves release a strong aroma (which sometimes suggests cat pee, but curiously is not unpleasant!). It is the ideal complement to tomatoes and pasta. Its purple-leaved variety with small pink flowers is used extensively in Thai or Vietnamese cooking; it has a more peppery flavor.

Bay

An essential ingredient of a bouquet-garni, bay has tough, pointed leaves that release a strong aroma. Their culinary use is well known, but you can also dry them and use them on the fire. In the past they were burned in places infested by the plague, because their smoke (like juniper smoke) was reputed to be disinfectant.

Benzoin

The name refers to the resin of an Asian tree. Once it has hardened, this resin produces 'tears' of benzoin, which burn like incense over charcoal. In addition, a tincture can be obtained from it, whose sweet, vanilla scent is very agreeable; added to bathwater, it softens the skin, and leaves it pleasantly perfumed. It is also used as a fixative for some potpourris, and you can add a few drops of it to sachets for scenting linen.

Cinnamon

Bergamot

This sort of inedible, thick-skinned orange provides an essence with a scent suggesting lemon, without the slightly acid flavor. In the eighteenth century its rind was used to make small boxes, whose lids were painted with decorative designs. Its oil is an ingredient of eau de cologne and many other perfumes, as well as delicious, slightly acid sweets—the bergamots of Nancy in France.

Camphor

A solid substance extracted from the wood of the camphor tree (a species of Asian laurel), camphor releases a strong aroma, somewhere between menthol and turpentine, whose prophylactic properties have been extensively used in pharmacists' drug manuals. It is one of the ingredients of certain ointments, such as the famous tiger balm. In Asia it is used as a moth repellent. In the past it was used to make cosmetic vinegars.

Cinnamon

This is the bark of the cinnamon tree, a small shrub originating from Ceylon, which is used in the form of sticks or is ground. Its pleasant, spicy perfume lends itself both to cooking (where its flavor can be appreciated in desserts) and to making potpourris, pomanders, and scented sachets (for these it is best to use ground cinnamon).

Cardamom

This plant, which belongs to the ginger family and originates in Asia, produces green, brown, or white seeds. Connoisseurs prefer green cardamom, with its more powerful aroma. The thicker, brown seeds are less fragrant; and the white ones (which are generally available commercially) are simply green seeds, blanched after treatment. They are valued in cooking, as well as in some potpourris, with a green scent. Chewing just a few seeds, removed from the fruit, will freshen the breath.

Chives and Spring Onions

These are two varieties of garlic. Chives (*Allium schoenoprasum*) resemble spring onions (*Allium fistulosum*), but they do not grow taller than 15cm (6in), whereas their cousins can reach 30cm (1ft); like their leaves, chives' aroma is subtler and they have a milder taste. Both varieties are delicious mixed with salads, soups, and soft fresh cheese.

Cardamom

Cloves

Tonka beans

Cloves

These are the floral buds of a small shrub originating in Indonesia. In cooking you stud onions for stews with cloves. In India cloves are among the ingredients of curry powders and garam masala. For a long time perfume makers used oil of cloves as a replacement for carnation oil, as it has a similar aroma. More recently they have substituted eugenol, a synthetic product that is easier to make in larger quantities. Cloves blend well with most potpourris and pomanders, and they are often included in the ingredients of certain spicy, scented sachets.

Elecampane

This perennial plant resembles a sunflower with velvety leaves. The root has many antiseptic properties. It contains a kind of natural starch, inulin, which once was known as the 'starch of the future,' because it was not expensive and was slightly aromatic. Once it has been cut into small pieces, it can be used in moth-repellent sachets or in laundry.

Geranium (*Pelargonium*)

Although these plants do flower, their blooms are often insignificant compared to the appeal of their fragrant leaves. The most well known is the pink geranium (*Pelargonium graveolens*), whose leaves with their lemony fragrance produce a very pronounced rose-scented essence, when they have been distilled. *Pelargonium tomentosum* has marvellous lobed, velvety leaves, giving off a strong peppermint aroma. The leaves of these two species are used for potpourris or sachets, and they are mixed with other leaves and flowers to make attractive scented bouquets.

Ginger

Ginger used in cooking is the root of an Asian plant, a cousin of the canna. Its aroma suggests both pepper and soap! Asians like to preserve it in sugar, for desserts, or pickle it in vinegar, where the thin strips take on a light pinkish tint. In potpourris it provides an interesting hint of pepper, but, like pepper, it should be used sparingly.

Geranium or pelargonium

Lavender

Mace and nutmeg

Iris

Contrary to what some people maintain, there are irises with a very strong, somewhat sweet and mauve fragrance, like wisteria. But in reality the only sought-after fragrance is the scent of the Florence iris, of which only the dry root is used. Once reduced to powder or transformed into 'iris butter' for perfumers, it releases a subtle and delicate fragrance of violets. Orris root powder acts as a fixative for potpourris, and can also be used as a natural toothpaste to whiten the teeth and freshen the mouth. Dry roots have been used since ancient times to perfume water for laundry washing.

Lavender

It grows in its wild state on high plateaux in the Provençal countryside, coloring the landscape with its unique blue, which is often combined with the gold of ripe wheat. It is the essential complement to clean linen, neatly put away in wardrobes. Bundles or sachets are made from it, because its pleasant fragrance has moth-repellent properties. You can also mix it with many other plants to make pot-pourris, and perfume your bathwater with its mauve seeds, wrapped in a muslin sachet. The most common is the *Lavandula officinalis* but the lavender known as *Lavandula stoechas*, with its floral bracts resembling mauve butterflies, has a very interesting flower, and a stronger, more camphor-like aroma.

Lemonbalm (melissa)

It shares with vervain and Asian citronella a lemon scent that can be detected when you rub its green, rounded, crinkled leaves between your fingers. Delicious as a tea, it has given its name to an aromatic alcoholic drink (melissa liqueur), taken for headaches and nausea. It enhances all potpourris with a green scent, and is also one of the ingredients of eau de cologne and perfumed sachets for linen.

Mace and Nutmeg

Mace is the membranous outer covering of the nutmeg, at the heart of a fruit collected from a tree originating in Indonesia. A kind of orangey, delicate, highly serrated bark, mace has a much heavier perfume than nutmeg, with its fine, subtle aroma. It is an ingredient of some mulled wines and liqueurs, while nutmeg is a wonderful complement to mashed potato and white sauces. Both are also used to enhance the fragrance of pomanders and some potpourris.

Marjoram or Oregano

This has a very similar scent to that of thyme, although marjoram smells stronger and slightly bitter, especially if the plant has grown in dry soil, in a sunny position. Its fresh or dried leaves are often set aside for culinary purposes (salads, cooked vegetables, grilled meats, pizzas), but when it comes into flower you can combine it with other plants to make bouquets. The dried leaves are sometimes used in sachets for linen.

Mint

There is not just 'one' mint, but an infinite number of varieties, which share the unmistakable scent, more or less green, peppery or lemony. There is garden mint, peppermint, or *Mentha pulegium* (also known by the pretty name pennyroyal). In ancient times it was already known that pennyroyal repelled fleas and its dried leaves were used as bedding for dogs (an idea that is still valid today).

Mint

Oak moss

Myrrh

This is a scented resin that oozes from the bark of *Commyphora myrrha*, a shrub that grows naturally in Yemen and Somalia; as it dries, the 'tears' of myrrh turn amber or reddish-brown. According to some, its aroma evokes lemon and rosemary, as it is both quite pungent and bitter. The Romans infused it in wine, to perfume it. It is burned over charcoal.

Neroli (Orange flower)

Orange flower is one of the ingredients of all fresh, scented waters, such as eau de cologne. Its name is what perfumers call the essential oil extracted from the blossom of the bitter orange or the Seville orange tree, which grows in Calabria and Sicily. You need 1 ton (1,000 kg; 2,200 lb) of freshly cut petals to obtain 1kg (2.2 lb) of pure essence after distillation with solvents. The plants distilled with steam produce orange flower water. The leaves are also used: they produce petit-grain essence, which has a bitter, greener fragrance, whereas neroli is very flowery.

Olibanum (Frankincense)

Its name comes from a distortion of the Arab word *lubân*, meaning 'white.' It is a scented resinous gum secreted by trees of the *Boswellia* genus growing in Africa, India, and Arabia. It is the finest incense, whose aroma and perfume have been sought since early antiquity. It is burned over charcoal.

Oregano

See marjoram.

Parsley

Among aromatic herbs, this is undoubtedly the most widely used in France. Like bay, it is one of the ingredients of a bouquet-garni. Although the very decorative, curly-leaved parsley is the most common, flat-leaf parsley with its incomparable flavor is always to be preferred. Its main use is in cooking, though it has several medicinal properties.

Pepper

Rosemary

Patchouli

This strange perfume, with its heady aroma, seems to have been the symbol of the 1960s, the hippie years, as there was so much use and misuse of the substance during this period, particularly in the form of incense. The oil is obtained from the dried and fermented leaves of a shrub grown in Indonesia, India, and China. In the past it was used as a moth repellent. Patchouli is available from certain herbalists; those who appreciate its perfume add it to sachets for scenting their clothes.

Pelargonium

See geranium.

Pepper

These are the seeds of the pepper tree (*Piper nigrum*), an exotic climbing vine. You find green, red, white, and black grains, with various flavors—it is the same seed but at different stages of maturity. Gourmets prefer black pepper to white pepper, and the curious seek out (in certain delicatessens) the elongated seeds of long-grained pepper (*Piper longum*) with its astonishing perfume, ideal for potpourris and scented arrangements.

Rosemary

Although rosemary is mainly known as an aromatic plant, reserved for cooking, in the past it was also one of the ingredients of perfumed waters such as the famous Queen of Hungary Water (a kind of eau de cologne, highly valued by Louis XIV), which would have preserved the youthfulness of Queen Elizabeth of Hungary. The Hungarian queen used to rub her body down with it and drink a few glassfuls, as if it were an alcoholic drink! With rosemary branches you can perfume bathwater, essential-oil water, and toilet vinegar. Or you can make large aromatic bouquets combining various types of foliage and flowers; once they have dried they will perfume the fire in your grate.

Sage

This plant is much used in cooking (especially added to white meats), but we sometimes overlook that it has superb, velvety, ash-grey leaves, and that when it comes into flower, it produces magnificent spikes of violet flowers, which can be used in bouquets. Clary sage, a giant of a plant, which can grow to more than 1m (3 feet) tall, is highly prized by perfumers for the heart or base note of a fragrance.

Thyme

Vanilla

Sandalwood

Mainly grown in India, particularly in Mysore, sandalwood has a bark that releases a warm perfume suggestive of leather. As this tree is in danger of extinction, its trade is highly regulated. Sandalwood has been used for thousands of years to make incense sticks, and its oil is one of the ingredients of many perfumes, for both men and women, with Oriental and woody drifts. Some herbalists still offer sandalwood shavings to be steeped in alcohol, vinegar, or oil, or to add to a woody potpourri and to sachets for scenting linen.

Santolina

Gardeners who create flowerbeds will be very familiar with this serrated, ash-grey and strongly aromatic herb with very fine leaves. It grows to the right height to define the boundaries of enclosed squares, such as were found in the gardens of the Middle Ages. Its aroma repels both moths and flies. It can be used to make scented sachets.

Star anise

Originating in China, the star anise tree is a small tree whose flowers yield star-shaped fruits with seven or eight points, each containing a small glistening seed. These stars, which look as if they have been cut from wood, release a very strong aniseed scent. They are used a lot in aperitif recipes such as pastis. In Chinese or Vietnamese cooking star anise perfumes beef dishes, and stocks. You can slip it into certain faintly woody potpourris or use it in table decorations.

Sweet-flag

This marsh plant has long, straight leaves, reminiscent of iris leaves. In the Middle Ages they were scattered over the floor to disinfect and perfume the air throughout houses. Their pleasant aroma evokes cinnamon. Pieces of the root are used in laundry washing and in some potpourris.

Sweet woodruff

This wild plant grows in some areas of undergrowth. When it is drying, its small white flowers release a lovely aroma of mown hay with a hint of vanilla, that perfume makers refer to as 'coumarin' (an aromatic crystalline substance). It is used to make a scented drink with white wine as its base, called May wine. Use it in scented sachets for linen or in your pillows, as its pleasant perfume encourages a restful night.

Tansy

Very popular in the past, this aromatic plant, cousin of the santolina and wild chrysanthemum, was used as a herb for seasoning dishes. Put into sachets intended for linen and cupboards, it is a moth repellent.

Thyme

In France thyme is, with bay and parsley, one of the three most popular aromatic herb and an essential ingredient of a bouquet-garni. Lemon thyme can feature in some green, leaf-based potpourris; it is a variety with leaves that are sometimes variegated, and has a delicious aroma.

Vetiver

Tonka beans

Produced by a Guyanan tree, tonka beans are black and shiny fruits. Perfume makers extract an essence from them known as coumarin (an aromatic crystalline substance—the name comes from the local name for the tree, the *coumaronà* or *coumaron*), with a very sweet, vanilla fragrance. In the past it was used to perfume certain tobaccos and its very individual scent is found in many great perfumes, such as Habanita by Molinard or L'Heure Bleue by Guerlain. You can use it to enhance potpourris and scented sachets.

Vanilla

This is the dried pod of the fruit of an orchid, with insignificant small flowers, which is grown in the regions of the Indian Ocean, especially in Réunion, in Madagascar or in Tahiti, but it originated in Mexico, where the Incas used it to perfume their chocolate. Its sweet, aromatic fragrance is useful both in cooking and in perfume making. For example, vanilla is a base note of Jicky, Shalimar, or L'Heure Bleue, legendary Guerlain perfumes.

Vervain

Originating in Central America, this straight-leaved plant with insignificant flowers has one of the most wonderful lemon perfumes of the plant world. You only need to immerse a single branch in a jug of fresh water to give it a delicious flavor. It is used in potpourris, sachets, scented water, and bathwater. Be careful with its oil, as it is an irritant when it comes into direct contact with the skin.

Vetiver

Only the roots of this plant, from the same family as the citronella and growing mainly in the regions of the Indian Ocean are used. The roots are sometimes used to make everyday objects such as blinds or fans. Their peculiarity is that they release the fullness of their fragrance, which is somewhat green and earthy, when they are moist. Vetiver is found in many after-shave lotions. In its original form it perfumes linen or livens up certain potpourris.

Wormwood

A cousin of tarragon, wormwood is sometimes known as one of the Midsummer's Day herbs, because it is collected in summer. Its highly serrated and feathery, ash-grey leaves have an aromatic scent with a tinge of bitterness. They are used to make scented posies, mixed with mint or absinthe. You can also use them in moth-repellent sachets.

Ylang-ylang

This magical flower blooms in the islands of the Indian Ocean, particularly in the islands of the archipelago of the Comoros, picturesquely known as the 'islands of the Moon.' Produced by the *Cananga odorata*, the flowers look like a sort of plant spider, of a greenish-yellow color, and they release a sweet, penetrating aroma. Ylang-ylang essence is obtained by distilling freshly cut flowers.

A small selection of addresses of sources of delicious ready-made products, if you have neither the time nor patience to prepare them yourself.

Aveda
locations throughout the U.S.
www.aveda.com

Much more than traditional beauty boutiques, Aveda stores emphasize complete beauty and wellness and promote a healthy, environmentally friendly lifestyle. In addition to flower and plant products, Aveda also sells air and body care products, tea, and aroma jewelry.

Barneys New York
660 Madison Avenue, New York, NY 10022
Tel: 212 473 0280
www.barneys.com

Barneys New York stocks an excellent range of products from established perfume houses. This is also a good place to find scented items for the home. Among other brands, Barneys carries a wide range of Kiehls products.

Bergdorf Goodman
754 Fifth Avenue, New York, NY 10019
Tel: 212 872 2522

This exclusive New York department store carries only the very best brands from the world's most established perfume houses.

The Conran Shop
Bridgemarket, 407 East 59th Street
New York, NY 10022
Tel: 212 755 9079
www.conran.com

In its continuing expansion, The Conran Shop, with its full range of home furnishings, offers a collection of scented goods to complement all the rooms in your home. In addition, a good selection of bath and beauty products are on offer. Maintaining the chic, modern, trademark look, Conran products are beautifully designed with a clean appearance, perfect for those wanting to give a contemporary feel to their home.

Crabtree & Evelyn
locations throughout the U.S.
Tel: 1 800 272 2873
www.crabtree-evelyn.com

Here you can find some of the best fragrances for the home, all in beautiful packaging. Only the finest essences, oils, and extracts are used to create a range of products, including scented candles, linen and room sprays, drawer liners, and potpourris, as well as bath and body products, all at modest prices. In addition, each product can be gift wrapped for a personal touch.

Diptyque
Selected department stores throughout the U.S.
www.diptyque.tm.fr

The extensive range of fragrances for home and body, including scented candles, room sprays, essential oils and soaps has become a great success for this French company. There are 43 different fragrances, inspired by nature, for the home.

Floris

70 Madison Avenue, New York, NY 10021
Tel: 212 935 9100
www.florislondon.com

As befits London's oldest perfumer, superior products with floral fragrances accompany Floris's renowned perfumes. A section for the home includes room fragrances and incense together with lamp vaporizer sets and silver-plated incense holders.

Fragonard

Selected department stores throughout the U.S.
www.fragonard.com

Since 1926, Fragonard has combined centuries-old traditions with modern production techniques. It produces and sells some of the finest French perfumes and soaps, each created from entirely natural ingredients.

Gracious Home

1992 Broadway, New York, NY 10023
Tel.: 212 231 7800
www.gracioushome.com

Gracious Home is known for its vast selction of fine foods as well as products for the home. There you will find everything from exotic blends of tea to candles and scents for every room of your home.

Kiehls

109 Third Avenue, New York, NY 10003
Tel: 212 677 3171
www.kiehls.com

Founded in 1851, Kiehls is in New York City's old-world pharmacy. Its unique and extensive background represents a blend of cosmetic, pharmaceutical, herbal, and medicinal knowledge developed through the generations. Here you can find all of their unique formulations for skin, hair, and body.

Jo Malone

The Flat Iron Building, 949 Broadway
New York, NY 10010
Tel: 212 673 2220
www.jomalone.co.uk

With a fabulous range of gifts for the home, Jo Malone offers a selection of exclusive own-brand products, including potpourris, luxurious room fragrances, and scented candles.

Neal's Yard Remedies

Selected department stores throughout the U.S.
www.nealsyardremedies.com

Best known for its haircare and skincare range packaged in classic blue glass bottles, Neal's Yard also stocks an extensive range of essential oils created for use in burners or for blending, base oils, scented candles, room spritzers, burners, and diffusers, as well as a range of accessories for creating and storing your products.

L'Occitane

510 Madison Avenue, New York, New York 10017
Tel: 212 826 5020
www.loccitane.com

L'Occitane perfumes and fragrances come from the hills of Provence in France, maintaining traditional customs and techniques in their methods. Renowned for its fine-quality products and high standards, its range for the home includes room fragrances and linen water—a delicate, refreshing scent for clothes and linen, suitable for use in steam irons.

Penhaligon's

Selected department stores throughout the U.S.
www.penhaligons.co.uk

With three royal warrants and recognized as one of the finest English perfume houses, Penhaligon's offers a timeless elegance to reflect its rich and established history. In addition to its individual bath and body products are room fragrances, egg-shaped candles, elegant snuffers, and a large selection of silver-plated candles.

Williams-Sonoma

locations throughout the U.S.
Tel: 1 800 541 2233
www.williams-sonoma.com

In keeping with Williams-Sonoma's ongoing search to find the best possible equipment for the home kitchen, they have developed a collection of aromatherapeutic necessities that complement food preparation rather than compete with it. These products include hand soaps, lotions, and cleaning products, each scented with essential oils of fruits or herbs.

Index – recipes

Index – general

Acknowledgements

The authors give special thanks to:
Marie-Annick Louis and Véronique Pauly
(The Conran Shop); Clarisse (Vertumne);
Caroline Régin-Pommier (Roger et Gallet);
Simon Carp (Christian Tortu) and Shapath
Colombel (Encens du Monde), for their
patience, kindness and all the information
they supplied; as well as Nathalie Bailleux
and Iris de Moüy. Without forgetting,
of course, all the people who lent them
objects and items for the photos. In order
of appearance in the book: Esteban, Muji,
Bô, Habitat, Terre de Sienne, Miller et
Bertaux, The Conran Shop, Sentou
Galerie, Christian Tortu, Orient and
China Company, P.M. and Co, N'Omades
Authentic, Quartz, Astier de Vilatte, Amin
Kader, Shiseido Perfumes, Dior Perfumes,
Roger et Gallet Perfumes, Résonances,
Vertumne, Fragonard, Édith Mézard,
La Paresse en Douce, Hermès, Mariage-
Frères, Côté-Bastide, Aurélia Fronty,
Luc Gaignard.

U.S. Edition:
Senior Editor: Elizabeth Smith
Jacket Designer: Amelia Costigan
Americanization: Ilaria Fusina

U.K. Edition:
Publishing Director: Lorraine Dickey
Senior Editor: Katey Day
Editorial Assistant: Sybella Marlow
Creative Director: Leslie Harrington
Creative Manager: Lucy Gowans
Jacket Designer: Megan Smith
Production Director: Adam Smith
Translated by Sara Harris in association
with First Edition Translations Ltd,
Cambridge, U.K.

French Edition:
Editors: Nathalie Bailleux
and Laurence Basset
Artistic supervision: Sabine Houplain
Design and production: Iris de Moüy
Proofreading: Isabelle Macé

Photoengraving QUADRILASER
Printed and bound in France by POLLINA,
Luçon - ISBN 0-7893-0687-5